INCREDIBLE CURIOSITIES - THE GREAT ATLAS OF WORLD MYSTERIES

TAKE A JOURNEY THROUGH THE SURPRISING SECRETS TO DISCOVER, LEARN AND ENJOY!

AURORA BRIGHTWOOD

EDITED BY
PURELEARN PUBLICATIONS

Incredible Curiosities - The Great Atlas of World Mysteries © Copyright 2024 by Aurora Brightwood (First Edition)

Copyrights

All contents of this book, including texts, quizzes, pictures, and illustrations, are protected by copyright laws. It is strictly forbidden to reproduce, distribute, or transmit any part of this book in any form or by any means, electronic or mechanical, including photocopying, recording, or any information storage and retrieval system, without the written permission of the publisher. The only exception permitted is the quotation of short extracts for review purposes.

Legal Notice

The information in this book is provided for educational and entertainment purposes only. It is not intended as a substitute for professional advice. While the author and publisher have worked to ensure the accuracy of the information contained herein, errors and omissions may occur. Neither the author nor the publisher shall be liable for any damages resulting from the use of this book.

This book was created with the intention of providing entertaining and educational information. Adult supervision is recommended when the book is used by children to ensure an appropriate and safe experience.

The contents of this book have been compiled with diligence and care, based on the author's knowledge and beliefs at the time of writing. However, it is recommended that qualified professionals be consulted before applying any of the information or suggestions provided.

The use of the information in this book is at the sole discretion of the reader. By continuing to read this book, the user accepts the conditions described and takes full responsibility for the decisions made based on its contents.

CONTENTS

Introduction   5

1. Science and Nature   11
2. Technology and Inventions   35
3. History and Culture   57
4. Geography and Places   81
5. World Records and Extraordinary Facts   99
   Conclusion: Beyond the Horizon   117

INTRODUCTION

HELLO THERE, YOUNG EXPLORERS!

Prepare yourselves for an enthralling voyage through the pages of our captivating book, Incredible Curiosities - The Great Atlas of World Mysteries. Imagine clutching a treasure map that leads you through enigmatic forests of facts, towering mountains of secrets, and vast oceans of knowledge.

INTRODUCTION

This book is a magical gateway that flings open the doors to hidden realms and troves of wisdom, letting you traverse the wide universe all from the snugness of your room. Each page whisks you away on a fresh escapade, where you'll unearth tales about fantastic creatures, amazing inventions, and the legacies of heroes and civilizations that have shaped our history.

Why Is This Book a Unique Treasure?

<u>A World of Knowledge at Your Fingertips:</u>

Plunge into the depths of the ocean, soar through starry galaxies, time-travel to ancient Egypt, or trek through lush rainforests—all without leaving your settee! This book is your ticket to a world brimming with astonishing curiosities and startling tales that will spark your curiosity and widen your view of the world.

<u>Fun That Ignites:</u>

Whoever said learning must be dull? Put your fresh knowledge to the test with interactive quizzes that make each discovery thrilling. You won't just soak up cool facts—you'll actively engage with them through brain-teasing questions that boost your memory. Compete with pals or family to see who can be crowned the champion of world mysteries!

<u>Think, Reflect, Grow:</u>

Every fact you uncover is like a building block for constructing your castle of critical thinking. You'll learn to scrutinize information, connect the dots between ideas, and dream up clever solutions to tricky problems. These vital skills will aid you at school and in day-to-day life, helping every reader to blossom into a sharp-witted thinker.

<u>An Enchanting Visual Experience:</u>

Each page bursts with vibrant, detailed illustrations that seize your imagination and deepen your understanding. The visuals transport you to different times and places, making each learning moment vivid and unforgettable.

<u>Quality Time Together:</u>

In a world ruled by screens, Incredible Curiosities provides a splendid chance to gather the whole family. Reading together, discussing the wonders you stumble upon, and tackling quizzes is a delightful and meaningful way to spend time together, strengthening family ties.

INTRODUCTION

<u>A Spark for Further Adventure:</u>

Just because you reach the last page doesn't mean your journey ends. Each curiosity fuels your desire to learn more, delve deeper, and keep questioning 'why' and 'how'. This thirst for knowledge is the essence of scientific and cultural exploration, and Incredible Curiosities is your launchpad for never-ending discovery.

Let's set off on this adventure together!

TREASURE MAP

Welcome to your Treasure Map! But this isn't just any old map scribbled on faded parchment; it's a detailed guide to the hidden marvels and wondrous secrets of our world.

<u>1. Science and Nature</u>

Pop on your naturalist's cap and your physicist's goggles, because this section is going to whisk you away to places beyond your wildest dreams. Delve deep into the ocean's abyss where peculiar creatures light up the darkness, and soar to the boundaries of space where time and light dance in a cosmic spectacle. Here, we'll uncover phenomena where science seems more like magic: from awe-inspiring weather events and the astonishing life cycles of dinosaurs to cutting-edge nature conservation tech.

2. Technology and Inventions

Step into a portal that transports you between the past and the future! Uncover how inventions have reshaped our world, from the ancient wheel to today's smartphones. Explore the realm of robotics, with machines learning to make decisions on their own, revolutionizing our ways of living and working. Discover the power of renewable energy that promises a greener tomorrow, and delve into some of humanity's quirkiest creations.

3. History and Culture

Take a time-travel adventure back to the dawn of civilizations, learning how ancient innovators built mighty empires and sparked cultural and technological revolutions that molded today's societies. This section is your time machine through history, uncovering the secrets of the Egyptian pyramids, the global influence of silk, and the concealed plots of revolutions that have reshaped our world.

4. Geography and Places

Our Earth is a patchwork of stunning landscapes and natural wonders ready for discovery. From enigmatic underwater cities to towering peaks that scrape the sky, every location tells its own epic story. Explore the vast deserts that stretch into the horizon and the complex network of biomes that sustain life in myriad forms across the globe.

5. World Records and Extraordinary Facts

Celebrate the incredible and the unimaginable in this section, where human endurance reaches new heights and natural phenomena challenge every bit of logic. Here, we salute the extremes of nature and the remarkable human spirit that continually pushes beyond the boundaries of the possible.

Each section of this book is like an island brimming with treasures, with paths you can follow in any order you choose, driven by your own curiosity and interests. Use this map to steer your journey, pick your path, and relish each discovery. The true treasure of this adventure lies in the knowledge and experiences you gather along the way.

So, grab your notebooks, young explorers! It's time to navigate these chapters and uncover the mysteries nestled in every corner of the book. Happy exploring, and let curiosity be your guide!

SCIENCE AND NATURE

SUPERHERO ANIMALS

Welcome to the superhero squad of the animal kingdom, where some creatures boast abilities so astonishing they could rival any comic book hero. These remarkable animals use their unique powers to navigate and thrive in their challenging habitats. Today, we're diving into a world where magic seems real and nature outshines fiction with its array of surprising capabilities, from mesmerizing camouflage to electrifying speed.

1. The Giant Salamander: The Queen of Regeneration

Picture this: what if you could regrow a lost limb or even mend your heart? The giant salamander has this remarkable ability. Should it lose a body part, it can regenerate it flawlessly, without even a scar to show. This amazing regenerative power offers clues to scientists, who study these creatures hoping to unlock new ways to heal injuries and cure diseases in humans.

2. The Uranus Butterfly: The Flying Camouflage Expert

Meet the Uranus butterfly, also known as Urania leilus, a master of disguise in the insect realm. Inhabiting the lush tropical forests stretching from Mexico to Brazil, this butterfly's wings dazzle with a vibrant metallic blue-green sheen when open. Yet, once closed, they transform to mimic the drab browns of dead leaves. This incredible dual appearance allows it to blend seamlessly into the foliage, eluding predators as it flits through the trees. It's like watching a leaf suddenly take flight—a truly spectacular sight!

3. The Camouflage Octopus: The King of Disguise

The camouflage octopus is a virtuoso in vanishing acts, capable of altering its skin's color and texture in just a blink. Thanks to specialized cells known as chromatophores, it can seamlessly blend into its surroundings, making itself nearly invisible. This swift change is a vital trick for dodging predators or ambushing unsuspecting prey.

4. The Peregrine Falcon: The Supersonic Pilot

Soaring as the speed champion of the skies, the peregrine falcon dives at breakneck speeds of up to 320 km per hour—surpassing the pace of a speeding race car! This phenomenal speed, combined with precision, allows it to swoop and capture its prey mid-flight, demonstrating aerial prowess that's hard to match.

5. The Golden Weaver Spider: The Yarn Engineer

Imagine a spider that spins a web of gold —stronger than steel and yet incredibly elastic. The golden weaver spider does just that. Its golden silk has the potential to revolutionize human technology, with applications ranging from ultra-light bulletproof vests to advanced surgical threads, helping humans mend wounds more effectively.

NATURE SHOWS

Nature is the grandest stage of all, hosting some of the world's most awe-inspiring and spellbinding performances. From celestial displays that stretch across the night sky to extraordinary terrestrial spectacles, these natural phenomena captivate our senses and ignite our urge to delve deeper into the mysteries of our planet. Let's journey together through some of these incredible natural wonders.

6. The Aurora Borealis: The Polar Light Ballet

Known as the northern lights, the aurora borealis is a mesmerizing light show visible in the polar skies. These ethereal lights are born when charged particles from the sun collide with the Earth's atmosphere. The sky bursts into a dance of colors—emerald greens, vivid reds, deep purples, and brilliant blues—forming a shifting curtain of light that enchants all who see it.

7. The Circumzenithal Arc: The Smile of Heaven

A rare and splendid sight, the circumzenithal arc resembles a rainbow that forms closer to the sun, high in the sky, not from rain but from ice crystals in cirrus clouds. This arc is often brighter and more vividly coloured than a typical rainbow, as the sunlight passing through the ice crystals enhances the separation of colors, painting a celestial smile across the heavens.

8. The Basalt Columns of the Giant's Causeway: The Paving of the Giants

At the Giant's Causeway in Northern Ireland, an array of tightly packed basalt columns forms an almost surreal natural pavement. These geometric marvels are the result of an ancient volcanic eruption, where molten lava cooled and crystallized rapidly into nearly perfect hexagonal pillars—a stunning testament to nature's geometric precision.

9. Mud Volcanoes: Cold Geysers Erupting

Unlike their fiery molten-lava-spewing counterparts, mud volcanoes offer a gentler but no less remarkable spectacle. These formations occur when methane gas mixes with subterranean water and sediment, creating mud that is forced upward by the gas pressure. This mud builds into mounds that periodically erupt in spectacular, chilly bursts. While they pose less danger than traditional volcanoes, mud volcanoes provide a fascinating glimpse into the dynamic processes beneath the Earth's surface.

HEROES OF ECOLOGY

The heroes of ecology are unsung champions, not draped in capes or hidden behind masks, but absolutely vital for maintaining the delicate balance of our ecosystems. From the vast blue oceans to the fertile soil beneath our feet, these heroes, big and small, play pivotal roles in sustaining our planet's health. Let's celebrate these remarkable creatures and their contributions to preserving our natural world.

10. Whales: Giants of the Sea that Fertilize the Oceans

Whales, the colossal guardians of the marine realms, are not just awe-inspiring in their size but are crucial to the ocean's wellbeing. As they dive deep and resurface, they cycle nutrients from the ocean depths to the surface waters. This vertical migration aids the growth of plankton, the foundation of the marine food chain, which also plays a significant role in capturing CO_2 from the atmosphere, helping mitigate climate change.

11. The Bees: Supreme Pollinators of the Plant World

Bees are the powerhouse pollinators of our ecosystem, vital for both agriculture and natural habitats. Approximately 70% of the crops we consume rely on bees for pollination. Their tireless work ensures the production of many fruits, vegetables, and nuts, enriching our diets and sustaining agricultural productivity. Without bees, the diversity of our natural flora would be severely diminished, leading to drastic consequences for the ecosystems they support.

12. The Beavers: Engineers of River Ecosystems

Known for their remarkable dam-building skills, beavers play a critical role beyond just creating homes for themselves. Their dams create ponds and wetlands that serve as rich habitats for a variety of species. These water bodies act as natural filtration systems that enhance water quality and help control floods, thereby maintaining healthy river ecosystems and benefiting countless plant and animal communities downstream.

13. The Elephants: Architects of the Forests

Elephants, the mighty architects of the forests and savannahs, are essential for ecological balance. By feeding on dense vegetation, they help maintain the right conditions for a variety of plants and trees to thrive. The seeds that pass through their digestive systems often germinate more successfully, making elephants crucial in supporting healthy and diverse plant populations across their habitats.

14. Earthworms: Guardians of the Soil

Earthworms are the unsung heroes of the soil, instrumental in decomposing organic material, which enriches the earth with vital nutrients and maintains its fertility. Their activity helps to aerate the soil, improving its structure and making it more hospitable for plant growth. This not only aids in agriculture but also supports healthy terrestrial ecosystems around the globe.

THE MICROSCOPIC WORLD

The microscopic world, though invisible to the naked eye, is a bustling universe teeming with life that is crucial to the health of our planet. This unseen world is filled with tiny organisms, each playing a vital role in sustaining ecosystems, influencing our climate, and maintaining Earth's natural cycles. Let's dive into the fascinating intricacies of this miniature world and uncover some of its most incredible inhabitants.

15. Plankton: Foundations of the Ocean Ecosystem

Plankton, comprising both tiny plant-like organisms (phytoplankton) and animal-like organisms (zooplankton), drifts through ocean currents and forms the backbone of marine food webs. These minuscule organisms feed everything from the smallest of fish to the largest whales. Remarkably, phytoplankton are also prolific oxygen producers, outdoing even the vast tropical forests in their photosynthetic output, thereby playing a key role in regulating atmospheric oxygen levels.

16. Oil-Eating Bacteria: Natural Cleaners of the Seas

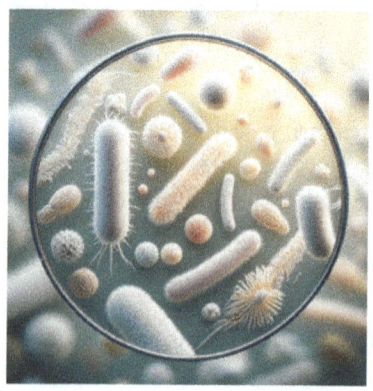

In the aftermath of oil spills, oil-eating bacteria are the unsung heroes that help mitigate environmental disasters. These bacteria break down hydrocarbons, the main components of oil, effectively cleaning up the spill by decomposing the oil into less harmful substances. Their natural biodegradation capabilities are essential for purifying water and reducing long-term ecological damage.

17. Mycetes: Mushroom Architects of the Soil

Mycetes, or fungi, are more than just decomposers of dead matter. They form vast underground networks known as mycorrhizae, which symbiotically connect with plant roots to enhance water and nutrient absorption. In exchange, plants supply fungi with carbohydrates produced through photosynthesis. This partnership is fundamental to the thriving of forests and other terrestrial ecosystems, helping maintain soil health and plant growth.

18. Viruses: Invisible Modellers of Evolution

Viruses, often only recognized for their role in causing diseases, are actually pivotal in shaping the evolutionary path of life. They facilitate horizontal gene transfer, which involves transferring genetic material between organisms, thus accelerating evolutionary changes and increasing genetic diversity. This mechanism has significant implications across various fields, including medicine, agriculture, and ecology, influencing how species adapt and evolve.

MYSTERIES OF THE UNIVERSE

The universe is an immense expanse filled with stars, planets, galaxies, and numerous mysteries that continue to perplex even the sharpest scientific minds. It beckons like a grand space odyssey, inviting us to venture forth and uncover celestial secrets that stretch our imaginations to their limits. Prepare to soar among the stars and delve into some of the cosmos's most captivating enigmas.

19. Black Holes: The Light Gobblers

Black holes are the cosmos's ultimate vacuum cleaners, engulfing everything in their path, including light itself! These enigmatic phenomena occur when massive stars collapse under their own gravity, creating regions in space where the gravitational pull is so intense that nothing, not even light, can break free. While black holes remain invisible to direct observation, scientists deduce their presence by studying their gravitational effects on nearby stars and gas clouds.

20. Galaxies: Cities of Stars

Galaxies are sprawling clusters of stars, dust, and gas, resembling gigantic cities in the celestial realm. Our own galaxy, the Milky Way, is home to up to 400 billion stars! While some galaxies dazzle with spiral arms swirling majestically around their centers, others appear as massive, star-filled spheres known as elliptical galaxies. Each galaxy is a microcosm of cosmic activity, hosting a myriad of stellar events and interactions.

21. Falling Stars: Illuminated Meteorites

Contrary to their name, 'shooting stars' are not stars at all but tiny bits of rock that ignite upon entering Earth's atmosphere. These meteorites become visible as streaks of light, heated by the friction of air molecules, as they plummet towards the ground. The tradition of making a wish upon seeing a shooting star adds a touch of magic to this stunning natural phenomenon, cherished by stargazers around the globe.

22. The Solar Eclipse: The Celestial Hiding Game

A solar eclipse is a fascinating cosmic event where the Moon aligns perfectly between the Earth and the Sun, cloaking the Sun in shadow. It's as though the Moon is playing a celestial game of hide-and-seek, momentarily hiding the Sun from view. This rare occurrence plunges the day into darkness and offers a unique spectacle that can be observed from specific regions on Earth.

SECRETS OF THE DEEP SEA

The deep sea is Earth's final frontier, a realm shrouded in perpetual darkness and icy waters, home to some of the most extraordinary creatures and phenomena that seem almost alien in nature. Let's plunge into the ocean's abyss and uncover the secrets that lurk in the shadows of the deep.

23. The Dragon's Teeth: Abyssal Fish with Glass Teeth

In the dark, crushing depths of the ocean, the dragonfish reigns with one of the animal kingdom's most curious adaptations—glass-like teeth. These teeth, clear and as sharp as razors, render the dragonfish's mouth nearly invisible, making it a formidable predator. This transparency is a perfect adaptation for a life in the pitch-black waters, allowing it to ambush its prey with lethal precision.

24. The Giant Squid: The Mysterious Giant of the Deep

The giant squid is a legendary denizen of the deep, stretching up to 13 metres —almost as long as a bus! Living in the profound depths, these squids are seldom seen by human eyes. They rely on their enormous eyes, some of the biggest in the world, to navigate the inky darkness of their deep-sea home.

25. The Cold Winds: Underwater Waterfalls

Among the ocean's most astonishing phenomena are the underwater waterfalls. These are not waterfalls in the traditional sense but are cold, dense water currents cascading down continental slopes, much like rivers beneath the sea. These currents are vital for distributing oxygen and nutrients to the remote reaches of the ocean floor, supporting life in these harsh environments.

26. The Underwater Mountains: Hidden Volcanoes

Beneath the ocean's surface, towering mountains and active volcanoes known as seamounts punctuate the seabed. Some are so active they occasionally erupt, creating new mountains or even islands. These submarine volcanoes are crucial in sculpting the ocean floor and fostering rich, diverse marine habitats.

EXTREME WEATHER PHENOMENA

Weather can display a breathtaking array of wild and wondrous behaviors! From tornadoes twisting across open lands to lightning that streaks the sky with brilliant flashes, extreme weather phenomena are not only mesmerizing spectacles but also key to understanding the dynamics of our planet.

27. Superstorms: Giants of the Sky

Superstorms, also known as supercells, are colossal storms that can unleash the most ferocious tornadoes and dazzling lightning displays. These meteorological giants are characterized by their internal rotation, known as a mesocyclone, making them highly organized and persistent. Capable of affecting vast areas, their incredible power showcases the intensity of Earth's atmospheric forces.

28. Tornadoes: The Wind Dancers

Tornadoes are spinning columns of air that connect the cloud base to the Earth. Resembling giant spinning funnels, they can wield enough force to lift and relocate heavy objects like cars and even houses. Tornadoes typically arise from severe thunderstorms when warm, moist air meets cooler, dry air, forming a violently rotating vortex.

29. Lightning of Catatumbo: The Continuous Light Show

The Catatumbo lightning, occurring over Venezuela's Lake Maracaibo, offers one of the most spectacular natural light shows on the planet. Nearly every night, this area lights up with thousands of lightning flashes that can last up to 10 hours. This phenomenon not only illuminates the night sky but also serves as a natural lighthouse, aiding navigation for ships.

30. Red Snow: The Coloured Mystery of the Poles

Red snow, or "watermelon snow," occurs primarily in polar regions and mountainous, cold climates. This phenomenon gets its distinctive color from a type of cold-loving algae that produces a red pigment to protect itself from ultraviolet light. The presence of this algae not only adds a splash of color to the icy landscapes but also plays a role in the melting patterns of snow and ice.

EXTRAORDINARY PLANTS

The world of plants is a veritable treasure trove of wonders and marvels. Some plants have developed astonishing abilities such as capturing insects, reacting to touch, or even emitting light in the dark! Beyond adding beauty to our planet, plants play crucial roles in purifying the air and providing vital resources for numerous life forms, including humans. Let's delve into the fascinating realm of some of the most extraordinary plants found on Earth.

31. The Venus Flytrap: The Insect-Eating Plant

The Venus Flytrap is a remarkable plant with a carnivorous twist—it eats insects! Its leaves snap shut swiftly when triggered by the touch of an unsuspecting victim. Equipped with tiny hair-like sensors, a mere double touch can cause the leaves to close, sealing the insect inside. The plant then secretes digestive enzymes, breaking down the insect to extract crucial nutrients.

32. The Sunflower: The Follower of the Sun

Known for its bright, large, sun-like blooms, the sunflower exhibits a unique behavior called heliotropism, where it turns its head to track the sun's journey across the sky. This movement ensures the plant receives ample sunlight throughout the day, aiding its growth and the vibrant display of its flowers.

33. The Mimosa Pudica: The Shy Plant

Mimosa Pudica, often called the shy plant, is notable for its rapid leaf movements in response to touch. When disturbed, the leaves fold inward and droop, a defense mechanism to deter potential herbivores. After some time, the leaves unfurl and resume their normal position, ready to react to the next threat.

34. The Dragon Tree: The Red Blood of Nature

The Dragon Tree is a striking figure native to the Canary Islands, famed for its 'blood'—a vivid red resin that exudes from its bark when cut. Historically, this resin has been utilized in varnishes, paints, and even medicine. The tree's unusual silhouette, featuring a stout trunk and a canopy of branches spreading almost horizontally, adds to its mystic allure.

35. The Bioluminescent Mushroom: Light in the Darkness of the Forest

In the quiet depths of the forest, bioluminescent mushrooms create a scene straight out of a fairy tale. These fungi emit a captivating blue-green glow, using light to attract insects that aid in dispersing their spores. Encountering these glowing mushrooms on a dark night is like stumbling upon a patch of earth sprinkled with fallen stars.

NOCTURNAL ANIMALS

As dusk falls and the world is shrouded in darkness, the enigmatic lives of nocturnal animals begin to unfold. These fascinating creatures have evolved remarkable adaptations to see, hunt, and navigate through the night, thriving during the hours when many of us are fast asleep. Let's explore the intriguing ways these animals have adapted to their nocturnal lifestyles and uncover the secrets they hold.

36. The Owl: The Great Eyes of the Night

Owls are renowned for their striking, luminous eyes that allow them to spot prey in nearly complete darkness. These large eyes are highly efficient at capturing even the faintest light, enhancing their night vision. Coupled with their extraordinary hearing, owls can detect the slightest movements—a rustling leaf or a scurrying mouse—making them formidable nocturnal hunters.

37. The Bat: The Flying Eco-Locator

Bats navigate the night skies with a remarkable ability known as echolocation. By emitting high-frequency sounds that bounce off objects and return as echoes, bats can determine the location, size, and even the texture of objects around them. This incredible sensory system allows them to dart through the air, skillfully avoiding obstacles and capturing insects on the wing.

38. The Desert Fox: The Ears of Silence

The desert fox, with its disproportionately large ears, uses its exceptional hearing to detect prey moving beneath the sand. These ears also serve a dual purpose by helping to dissipate heat, keeping the fox cool during the hot desert nights. The sensitivity of their hearing allows them to locate even the subtlest vibrations, giving them a crucial advantage in their arid, sparse habitats.

SCIENCE AND NATURE   23

39. The Badger: The Night Architect

Badgers are the diligent architects of the animal kingdom, known for constructing elaborate networks of burrows called setts. These nocturnal foragers use their powerful claws to dig extensive tunnel systems where they reside and seek refuge. At night, they emerge to hunt for a varied diet, ranging from earthworms and small mammals to berries and roots.

40. The Prairie Wolf: The Singer Under the Stars

Prairie wolves, or coyotes, are not wolves at all but highly social creatures that communicate through distinctive howls. These vocalizations serve multiple purposes: signaling danger, calling to potential mates, or maintaining the cohesion of their packs. Active primarily at night, the haunting calls of prairie wolves are a common sound in many North American landscapes, echoing under the moonlight.

UNUSUAL ECOSYSTEMS

Our planet is a canvas of incredible and diverse ecosystems, some so surreal and unique that they seem more like scenes from a science fiction novel than reality. These extraordinary places demonstrate nature's boundless creativity and adaptability. Let's explore some of the most unusual and mesmerizing ecosystems Earth has to offer.

41. The Coloured Mountains: The Painted Desert

In the heart of Peru lies Vinicunca, also known as Rainbow Mountain, a stunning natural wonder characterized by its vibrant, multi-colored hues. The mountain's striking colors are due to various mineral deposits: iron oxide imparts rich reds, copper lends greens, among others. This breathtaking landscape resembles a painter's palette, drawing both tourists and scientists eager

42. The Crystal Caverns: Underground Wonders

Beneath an ancient mine in Mexico lies the Crystal Cave, a subterranean marvel known for its enormous selenite crystals, some of the largest of their kind, reaching lengths of up to 12 metres. The cavern's extreme conditions—intense heat and high humidity—are perfect for the formation of these spectacular crystals, making it a fascinating, though challenging, site for exploration and study.

43. The Underwater Gardens of Coral: Forests in the Sea

Coral gardens thrive in the shallow, warm waters of tropical seas and are composed of corals that construct intricate limestone skeletons, forming the foundation of a richly biodiverse marine habitat. These underwater forests are not only stunningly beautiful but are vital to the health of the ocean, providing food, shelter, and breeding grounds for thousands of marine species.

44. The Petrified Forest: Trees Transformed into Stone

Arizona's Petrified Forest features remnants of ancient trees that over millions of years have transformed into stone through a process of permineralization. Minerals, particularly silica, seeped into the porous wood, replacing the organic material while retaining the original structure of the trees. Today, this national park showcases a surreal landscape of vibrant, multicolored petrified wood that offers a window into the deep geological past of our planet.

INCREDIBLE ANIMAL ADAPTATIONS

Animals across the globe have honed incredible abilities that allow them to thrive in the most extreme environments imaginable. These remarkable adaptations not only highlight the resilience of these creatures but also illustrate nature's genius in crafting solutions to a wide array of ecological challenges. Let's explore how some animals have evolved into true masters of adaptation.

45. The Camel: Survivor of the Desert

The camel, often referred to as the ship of the desert, is exceptionally adapted to survive the harsh conditions of arid landscapes. It can guzzle up to 100 liters of water in just one session, preparing it for long periods without hydration. Camels can also endure significant fluctuations in temperature, crucial in environments where daytime heat can be blistering and nighttime temperatures plummet. Furthermore, their thick eyelashes and specialized eyelids protect their eyes from  sand, while their wide, padded feet allow easy navigation across soft, shifting sands.

46. The Polar Bear: The Ice Giant

Polar bears are marvelously adapted to the freezing climes of the Arctic. Their fur, although appearing white, is actually transparent and hollow, trapping heat effectively. Beneath this insulating fur lies a layer of black skin that absorbs and retains solar heat, complemented by a thick layer of fat that provides buoyancy and insulation. The bear's large paws distribute its weight when walking on ice or snow, functioning like natural snowshoes.

47. The Toucan: The Colourful Beak Carrier

The toucan is instantly recognizable by its large, vibrant beak—a feature that's not just for show but highly functional. This oversized beak is surprisingly lightweight yet sturdy, enabling the toucan to reach fruits on slender branches far too weak to support its body weight. This adaptation allows the toucan to access food sources unavailable to other birds.

48. The Glass Frog: The Invisible of the Jungle

The glass frog possesses an extraordinary form of camouflage: transparency. With skin so clear that its internal organs are visible, this frog blends seamlessly into its leafy surroundings. This natural invisibility cloak provides superb protection from predators as it perches, nearly undetectable, among the foliage of the rainforest.

UNIQUE LIFE CYCLES

The life cycles of animals are as varied and fascinating as the creatures themselves. Some of these cycles are so unique and extraordinary, they truly highlight the wonders of nature, from dramatic transformations and epic journeys to near-immortal existences. Let's delve into some of the most captivating life cycles in the animal kingdom.

49. The Monarch Butterfly: The Air Traveller

The Monarch butterfly's life cycle encompasses one of the most awe-inspiring migrations of any insect species. Beginning life as a minuscule egg, it transforms into a voracious caterpillar, and later retreats within a cocoon to emerge as a vibrant butterfly. These butterflies undertake an epic journey spanning thousands of kilometers from Canada to Mexico annually—a migratory pattern that remarkably continues across generations.

50. The Salmon Life Cycle: The Countercurrent Swimmer

Salmon have a poignant and extraordinary life cycle that sees them migrating from the ocean depths back to their natal freshwater birthplaces to spawn. Navigating upstream, they overcome formidable obstacles and currents, driven by an unyielding instinct to return to where they were born. After spawning, their life cycle concludes tragically yet beautifully with their death, a sacrifice that ensures the continuation of their species.

51. The European Eel: The Mystery of the Oceans

The life cycle of the European eel remains one of the natural world's great mysteries. Born in the remote Sargasso Sea, these eels traverse thousands of kilometers to the freshwater rivers of Europe, maturing along the way. After many years, they return to the Sargasso Sea to spawn and end their life journey. The eel's elusive breeding habits and incredible migratory patterns continue to puzzle and fascinate scientists.

52. The Immortal Medusa: The Secret of Eternal Youth

The Turritopsis dohrnii, or the immortal jellyfish, possesses an almost mythical life cycle that defies the very nature of aging. Upon reaching maturity or encountering severe stress, this jellyfish can revert to its polyp stage, effectively beginning its life anew. This unique form of biological immortality, where it can cyclically revert from adult back to juvenile form, has made it a focus of scientific research into aging and regenerative biology.

DINOSAURS AND FOSSILS

Step into a time machine as we journey back millions of years to an era when dinosaurs, the titans of prehistory, roamed the Earth. While these magnificent creatures have long since vanished, they've left behind fossils that offer us a window into a world vastly different from our own. Let's explore some of the most intriguing dinosaurs and the secrets locked within their ancient remains.

53. The Tyrannosaurus Rex: King of Dinosaurs

The Tyrannosaurus Rex, often shortened to T-Rex, stood as one of the most formidable predators ever to walk the Earth. With its massive, banana-sized teeth and an incredibly powerful bite, it could crush bone with ease. Despite its comically short arms, the T-Rex was a terror to other dinosaurs, armed with a keen sense of smell and surprising speed that made it a relentless hunter.

54. The Triceratops: The Horned Defender

The Triceratops is easily recognized by its three distinct horns and a large, bony frill protecting its neck. These large herbivores likely moved in groups and used their horns for defense against predators like the T-Rex, as well as in combat with each other during the mating season, showcasing a blend of communal living and fierce individual combativeness.

55. The Apatosaurus: The Gentle Giant

Formerly known as the Brontosaurus, the Apatosaurus was a colossal dinosaur, reaching lengths of over 20 meters. This gentle giant was a herbivore, using its lengthy neck to browse high trees for foliage. Living in herds, the Apatosaurus relied on the safety of numbers to protect against predators, illustrating the social behaviors that contributed to their survival.

56. Archaeopteryx: The Bridge Between Dinosaurs and Birds

The Archaeopteryx fossil is pivotal in the study of evolutionary biology, showing a clear transitional link between dinosaurs and modern birds. This small creature had feathered wings akin to those of birds but retained many dinosaur-like features, such as sharp teeth and a long tail, offering critical insights into the evolutionary path that led to today's birds.

57. The Velociraptor: The Agile Predator

Popular culture often misrepresents Velociraptors as large, scaly monsters, but in reality, they were about the size of a turkey and covered in feathers. These agile predators were likely very intelligent and hunted in packs, using their sharp, sickle-shaped claws to tackle prey much larger than themselves, demonstrating that in the ancient world, cunning and teamwork often trumped sheer size.

THE HUMAN BODY

The human body is a marvel of nature, an intricate system where every part, from your hair to your toenails, plays a crucial role. Whether it's keeping us alive, helping us interact with the world, or even healing itself, our bodies are continuously working in remarkable ways. Let's explore some of the most incredible and interesting aspects of the human body.

58. The Heart: The Pump of Life

Our heart, the tireless pump within us, beats approximately 100,000 times each day, circulating blood throughout the body. This blood delivery system is vital, carrying oxygen and nutrients to every cell and ensuring that other organs have the energy they need to function. Without the heart's rhythmic beating, life would not persist as it delivers the essentials for our organs' survival.

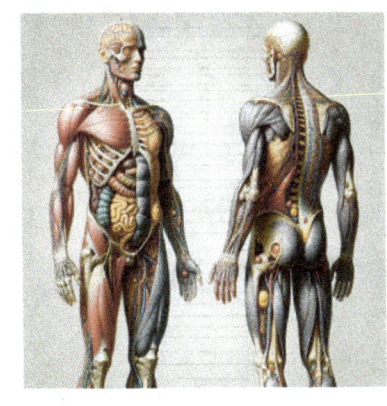

59. The Lungs: The Air Sacks

Think of the lungs as expansive air bags, inflating with every breath we take—around 20,000 breaths daily! They play a crucial role in our respiratory system, taking in oxygen from the air we inhale and expelling carbon dioxide, a waste product of metabolism, with every exhale. It's like having an internal cleansing service working tirelessly to keep our bodies fresh and free of unwanted gases!

60. The Brain: The Chief of Command

The brain is the master control center of the body, overseeing everything from the storage of precious memories to the physical motions involved in sprinting. Active 24/7, it continues to work hard even as we sleep, processing information and consolidating memories. The brain's importance is underscored by its protective housing—the skull, which acts as a fortified case to guard against injuries.

61. The Eyes: The Windows of the World

Our eyes are our personal windows to the world, functioning similarly to cameras. They capture light and convert it into images that our brain can interpret. Additionally, our eyes are equipped with a natural maintenance system—tears, which not only lubricate but also cleanse the eyes, ensuring that dust and debris are washed away with every blink.

62. The Skin: The Protective Cloak

The skin, our body's largest organ, serves as a protective barrier shielding our internal structures and helps us sense the world through touch. It's also pivotal

in regulating our body temperature, ensuring that we stay neither too hot nor too cold. Moreover, the skin is incredibly self-sufficient, capable of healing itself from minor cuts and scrapes through a sophisticated process of repair and regeneration.

TECHNOLOGIES FOR NATURE CONSERVATION

In our modern world, technology isn't just a tool for entertainment or completing homework—it's also a crucial ally in protecting the environment. Advanced technologies are now being harnessed to monitor endangered wildlife, cleanse our air, and generate clean energy, all contributing to the preservation of our planet. Let's explore some of the groundbreaking technologies making a significant impact on nature conservation.

63. Drones for Nature: Eyes in the Sky

Drones, or unmanned aerial vehicles (UAVs), are being increasingly deployed by conservationists as vigilant "eyes in the sky." These high-flying devices enable scientists to monitor vast expanses of nature—from sprawling forests to secluded turtle nesting beaches—without disturbing the habitat. Drones are invaluable for tracking illegal logging activities, spotting endangered species, and assessing the health of ecosystems, making them essential tools in the fight to protect our natural world.

64. Rubbish Collecting Robots: The Cleaners of the Oceans

Innovative robots designed to tackle pollution are taking to the seas to combat one of the most pressing environmental issues: oceanic plastic waste. These robots are programmed to navigate waters autonomously, scooping up plastic debris and other pollutants. Their work is vital for maintaining clean oceans, thereby protecting marine life from the dangers of ingested or entangled waste.

SCIENCE AND NATURE 31

These robots not only help clean our waters but also gather data that can lead to better waste management practices on land.

65. Solar Energy: The Power of the Sun

Solar energy, harnessed through panels that convert sunlight directly into electricity, represents a pinnacle of clean energy technology. This renewable energy source is crucial for reducing reliance on fossil fuels, which are major contributors to global warming. Solar panels produce no pollutants or greenhouse gases, offering a sustainable and eco-friendly energy solution. As solar technology advances and becomes more affordable, it holds the promise of a significantly cleaner and more sustainable planet.

QUIZ: TEST YOUR KNOWLEDGE ON SCIENCE AND NATURE

Question 1: What enables the camouflage octopus to change skin colour and shape?

- A) Sunlight
- B) Chromatophores
- C) Echolocation
- D) Bio-luminescence

Question 2: What is the maximum speed the Peregrine Falcon can reach while hunting?

- A) 160 km/h
- B) 240 km/h
- C) 320 km/h
- D) 400 km/h

Question 3: What is the special characteristic of the Uranus butterfly that allows it to camouflage itself during flight?

- A) It has wings that change colour from blue to red in flight.

- B) It can fly faster than any other insect.
- C) It has wings that look like dead leaves when closed.
- D) Make a sound that confuses predators.

Question 4: What natural phenomenon is known as 'The Polar Light Ballet'?

- A) The Circumzenital Rainbow
- B) The Aurora Borealis
- C) The Catatumbo Lightning
- D) The Solar Eclipse

Question 5: Why are whales considered important to the marine ecosystem?

- A) They produce oxygen
- B) Fertilise water with nutrients
- C) They consume large quantities of plastic
- D) They create sea currents

Question 6: What is the special feature of the Immortal Medusa?

- A) Can live without water
- B) Can turn into a polyp
- C) It feeds on plastic
- D) It emits light in the dark

Question 7: What do 'shooting stars' consist of?

- A) Glowing gas
- B) Cosmic rays
- C) Burning rocks
- D) Luminescent raindrops

Question 8: What does the Sunflower do during the day?

- A) Change colour
- B) Releases perfume
- C) Follows the sun
- D) Closing

SCIENCE AND NATURE

Question 9: Which animal is known for its ability to echolocate?

- A) The owl
- B) The toucan
- C) The Bat
- D) The Glass Frog

Question 10: What is the main function of earthworms in the ecosystem?

- A) Pollination
- B) Decomposition of organic matter
- C) Water purification
- D) Photosynthesis

ANSWERS:

- Question 1: B) Chromatophores
- Question 2: C) 320 km/h
- Question 3: C) It has wings that look like dead leaves when closed
- Question 4: B) The Aurora Borealis
- Question 5: B) Fertilise water with nutrients
- Question 6: B) Can it turn into a polyp
- Question 7: C) Burning rocks
- Question 8: C) Follows the sun
- Question 9: C) The bat
- Question 10: B) Decomposition of organic matter

TECHNOLOGY AND INVENTIONS

CRAZY MACHINES

Human creativity truly knows no bounds, especially when it comes to devising some of the most whimsical and astonishing machines. From the realm of science fiction to our everyday streets, these inventions showcase the fun and wild side of technology. Let's take a closer look at some of the craziest and most incredible machines that have sprung from human ingenuity.

66. Jetpacks: Backpacks That Make You Fly

Imagine strapping on a backpack, not to carry books, but to fly through the sky! Jetpacks transform this fantasy into reality. Powered by engines that thrust air downwards, these amazing devices allow individuals to soar above the ground, bypass traffic, and experience the thrill of flight. Whether it's zooming past cityscapes or leaping over landscapes, jetpacks bring a new dimension to personal travel and adventure.

67. Customised Underwater Vehicles: Explore the Seabed

For those who dream of exploring the ocean's depths but lack diving skills, customised underwater vehicles are the perfect solution. These personal submarines allow users to glide through underwater environments, closely observing marine life, intricate coral reefs, and submerged mysteries. Safe, comfortable, and equipped with the latest technology, these vehicles provide a unique window into the vast, often unexplored aquatic world.

68. Driverless Cars: Self-driving Cars

Driverless cars are transforming the way we think about travel. Equipped with advanced sensors, cameras, and AI, these autonomous vehicles navigate roads, make decisions about speed and direction, and adapt to real-time traffic conditions—all without human input. These self-driving cars promise a future where commuting is less about stress and more about relaxation, efficiency, and safety. They symbolize a significant leap forward in merging robotics with everyday life, potentially making roads safer and journeys more comfortable.

RECORD-BREAKING INVENTORS

Behind every transformative invention, there stands an inventor whose brilliant ideas have reshaped the way we live. These inventors not only introduced new ways of thinking but also created groundbreaking technologies that continue to influence our lives to this day. Let's explore the stories of some of the most prolific inventors who have left an indelible mark on history.

69. Thomas Edison: The Man Who Enlightened the World

Thomas Edison remains one of the most iconic figures in the annals of innovation, renowned for bringing electric light to the masses. His development of the practical electric light bulb revolutionized indoor lighting, moving the world away from candles and oil lamps. However, Edison's genius didn't stop at illumination; he held over 1,000 patents and made significant improvements in sound recording with the phonograph and in motion pictures through his work on the cinema projector. His inventions fundamentally changed how we interact with media and experience the world around us.

70. Wright Brothers: The Fathers of Modern Flight

Orville and Wilbur Wright, better known as the Wright brothers, are credited with inventing and flying the world's first successful motor-operated airplane. Their historic flight in 1903 at Kitty Hawk, North Carolina, marked the beginning of the age of aviation. This breakthrough made it possible to traverse vast distances in significantly less time, connecting people and cultures in unprecedented ways and ushering in a new era of global exploration and interaction.

71. Alexander Graham Bell: The Inventor of Distance Dialogue

Alexander Graham Bell's invention of the telephone dramatically transformed personal and business communication by enabling people to speak with each other in real-time across great distances. Introduced in 1876, the telephone quickly became an indispensable tool for communication, laying the groundwork for the connected world we live in today. Bell's work opened up new avenues for rapid and effective communication, proving crucial for both everyday and emergency interactions.

72. Nikola Tesla: The Wizard of Electricity

Nikola Tesla was a visionary inventor and electrical engineer who made extraordinary contributions to the development of electrical engineering. His pioneering work on alternating current (AC) systems forms the basis of modern electrical supply systems, powering industries, cities, and homes. Tesla's inventions went beyond AC, as he delved into early theories of radio and radar and

experimented with wireless transmission of energy, exploring technological possibilities that were far ahead of his time.

ADVANCED ROBOTICS

Advanced robotics is revolutionizing our capabilities, pushing the boundaries of what machines can do in environments that range from outer space to operating rooms. These innovations are not just changing the landscape of possibility but are also enhancing safety, efficiency, and precision in various fields. Let's delve into some of the most groundbreaking robotic inventions that are reshaping our world.

73. Mars Explorers: Robots Walking on Other Planets

Mars rovers, the robotic explorers of the Red Planet, have become crucial in our quest to understand our celestial neighbor. These sophisticated machines traverse the Martian surface, gathering data and snapping pictures that are sent back to Earth. This information has been invaluable in assessing the planet's past habitability and continues to fuel discussions about potential life on Mars as well as future human missions.

74. Rescue Drones: Flying Guardian Angels

Rescue drones represent a significant advancement in emergency response technology. Deployed in scenarios like earthquakes, floods, or other disasters, these drones swiftly locate and assist people in distress. Capable of reaching areas that are otherwise inaccessible or too dangerous for human responders, rescue drones are becoming indispensable in disaster management, significantly improving chances of survival and efficient resource allocation.

75. Robot Surgeons: The Doctors of the Future

Robot surgeons are transforming modern medicine by assisting doctors in performing precise and minimally invasive surgeries. These robotic systems offer exceptional dexterity and control beyond human capabilities, allowing for operations that are less invasive, significantly reducing recovery time and improving surgical outcomes. As technology advances, these robots are set to

TECHNOLOGY AND INVENTIONS

become even more integrated into various medical procedures, heralding a new era of surgical care.

76. Robot Farmers: The Farmers of Tomorrow

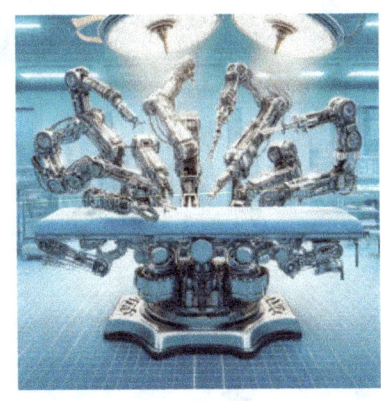

In the agricultural sector, robot farmers are making farming more sustainable and efficient. These robots handle tasks from planting seeds to watering and harvesting crops, operating around the clock to ensure optimal plant care. They precisely administer water and nutrients, reducing waste and increasing yield. This shift not only addresses labor shortages but also plays a crucial role in meeting the growing food demands of the global population.

SPACE TRAVEL

Exploring space is one of the most exciting adventures that technology and human invention have ever undertaken. From rockets hurtling past Earth's atmosphere to space stations where astronauts live and work, every aspect of space travel is filled with technological marvels. Let's take a look at some of the most extraordinary innovations that allow us to explore the stars.

77. The International Space Station: A Home among the Stars

The International Space Station (ISS) is like a big laboratory orbiting the Earth. Astronauts from all over the world come here to do experiments they could not do on Earth, study how to live in space, and look at our planet from a whole new perspective. It is a piece of human home floating in the vacuum of space.

78. Reusable Rockets: Flying, Landing, and Flying Again

Reusable rockets are a great invention that changes the way we think about space travel. Instead of using a rocket only once, these technological marvels can return to Earth, land safely and be prepared for another trip. This makes space travel much less expensive and opens up new possibilities for exploring space more often.

79. Space Telescopes: The Eyes that Look at the Universe

Space telescopes, such as the famous Hubble, are incredible instruments that orbit the Earth and look further into space than we can imagine. They have shown us images of stars being born, distant galaxies and even planets in other solar systems. They are like time machines that show us how the universe looked millions of years ago.

80. Space Suits: Clothes for the Universe

Space suits are more than just clothes. They are designed to protect astronauts from extreme space, where there is no air and temperatures can be incredibly hot or cold. These suits keep astronauts safe by regulating temperature,

providing oxygen, and even protecting them from the sun's harmful rays.

TRANSPORT OF THE FUTURE

As we look toward the future, the way we travel is evolving in astonishing ways, harnessing new technologies to make our journeys faster, more efficient, and environmentally friendly. These innovations promise not just to change how we move from point A to point B but to transform our entire experience of exploration and travel. Let's dive into some of the most cutting-edge and thrilling transport technologies that could soon become a part of our everyday lives.

81. Amphibious Cars: From Road to Water without Changing Vehicle

Amphibious cars blur the lines between automobile and boat, offering seamless transitions from land to water. Perfect for coastal areas and regions crisscrossed by waterways, these vehicles allow you to drive along the road and then continue your journey across water, exploring lakeshores and riverbanks without ever leaving the comfort of your car. This dual functionality makes them ideal for adventure and utility alike.

82. Hyperloop: The Super Fast Train

Envisioned by innovators like Elon Musk, the Hyperloop represents the next leap in transport technology—a train system that propels passenger pods through low-pressure tubes at speeds comparable to aircraft. This ultra-fast train could drastically reduce travel times between major cities, making it possible to commute between places like Los Angeles and San Francisco in under 30 minutes. The reduction of air friction allows these pods to glide at phenomenal speeds, revolutionizing intercity travel.

83. Personal Flying Vehicles: The Dream of Flying Realised

Once a fantasy confined to science fiction, personal flying vehicles are becoming a reality. These vehicles, ranging from hoverbikes to flying cars, offer individual or duo travel above traffic, dramatically cutting down commute times and redefining personal mobility. As these technologies advance, we might soon see skies filled with commuters piloting their own vehicles to work, vastly expanding the dimensions of everyday travel.

84. Tourist Submarines: Exploring the Mysteries of the Sea

TECHNOLOGY AND INVENTIONS 43

Tourist submarines open up the underwater world to exploration and adventure, allowing passengers to journey into the depths of the oceans safely and comfortably. These vessels can visit shipwrecks, dive along coral reefs, or observe deep-sea marine life in its natural habitat, providing a window into the mysterious aquatic world that covers the majority of our planet.

85. Magnetic Levitation Trains: Floating Over the Tracks

Magnetic levitation trains, or maglev trains, utilize powerful magnetic forces to lift and propel the train forward without direct contact with the track. This technology allows for smoother and faster travel at speeds that rival or exceed traditional high-speed trains, revolutionizing rail travel by reducing friction and increasing efficiency.

RENEWABLE ENERGIES

Renewable energy sources are essential for a sustainable future, offering us ways to generate power without depleting resources or harming our planet. The earth provides us with various natural elements that can be harnessed to produce clean energy. From the force of the wind and water to the heat beneath our feet, let's explore how these incredible resources are transformed into electricity that powers our daily lives while keeping our environment intact.

86. Wind Turbines: The Wind Giants

Wind turbines, towering and majestic, are modern-day windmills that harness the kinetic energy of the wind. These structures are equipped with large blades that rotate when the wind blows, converting wind energy into electrical energy through a generator housed within the turbine. On breezy days, they can generate significant amounts of clean energy, contributing to our power supply without any pollution. They stand idle on calm days, but when the wind picks up, they become powerful tools in the fight against climate change.

87. Hydroelectricity: The Power of Water

Hydroelectric power plants are incredible installations that convert the energy of flowing water into electricity. Water stored in a reservoir is released through dams, rushing down to spin large turbines. This process is similar to creating a massive whirlpool that powers a dynamo, producing electricity as the water flows. Hydroelectricity is one of the most established forms of renewable energy and is especially powerful because water flow can be controlled and is relatively consistent.

88. Geothermal: Heat from the Earth

Geothermal energy taps into the heat stored beneath the Earth's surface. This heat can be very close to the surface in geologically active regions, like Iceland, where it's used to heat water and buildings and generate electricity.

TECHNOLOGY AND INVENTIONS

Geothermal plants convert this subterranean heat into usable energy, offering a reliable and sustainable energy source that doesn't rely on weather conditions, unlike other renewable sources. It's like using the Earth's inner heat as a giant, natural furnace that runs continuously, providing a stable supply of energy.

ACCIDENTAL INVENTIONS

The path to innovation isn't always straightforward. Many of our everyday conveniences were born not through intentional design, but through happy accidents that occurred when scientists and inventors were aiming for something entirely different. These serendipitous discoveries remind us of the unexpected ways in which significant advances can arise. Here are some of the most interesting and impactful inventions that came about by chance:

89. Post-it Notes: The Perfect Sticker for Mistakes

In a classic tale of accidental invention, Post-it Notes emerged when Spencer Silver, a scientist at 3M, attempted to develop a super-strong adhesive. Instead, he created a low-tack, reusable adhesive. His colleague, Art Fry, realized its potential for a non-damaging bookmark, and thus, the Post-it Note was born. This seemingly simple product revolutionized note-taking and organization, demonstrating how a failed experiment can turn into a ubiquitous office tool.

90. Penicillin: A Most Important Discovery

Penicillin, the world's first antibiotic, was discovered purely by accident. Alexander Fleming, a bacteriologist, observed that a mold, Penicillium notatum, had contaminated one of his petri dishes and was killing the surrounding bacteria. This chance observation led to the development of penicillin, which has saved countless lives from bacterial infections since its introduction, marking a major breakthrough in medical history.

91. The Microwave: Rapid Heating

The microwave oven owes its existence to another accidental discovery by Percy Spencer, an engineer working on radar technology. He noticed that a candy bar in his pocket had melted while he was experimenting with a magnetron, a type of vacuum tube. This led him to experiment further with microwaves, ultimately resulting in the development of the microwave oven, a staple in kitchens around the world for its speed and convenience in heating food.

92. Velcro: Sticky Like a Plant

Velcro was inspired by nature and discovered through personal curiosity. George de Mestral, a Swiss engineer, observed how burrs from the burdock plant clung to his clothes and his dog's fur due to their tiny hooks. Seeing the potential for a new type of fastener, he developed Velcro, a hook-and-loop fastener that mimicked this natural adherence mechanism. Velcro is now widely used in clothing, footwear, and many other applications.

COMPUTER HISTORY

Computers have radically transformed nearly every aspect of our lives, evolving from complex mechanical devices to essential tools that assist in a multitude of tasks including education, work, and entertainment. The journey of the computer from its inception to its current state is a fascinating story of innovation and ingenuity. Let's delve into some key milestones that have defined this evolution.

93. The Mechanical Computer: The Ancestor of Computers

The journey into the history of computers begins with the mechanical calculator, known as the Pascaline, invented by Blaise Pascal in 1642. This device, crafted from gears and wheels, was developed to assist his father with arithmetic needed for his job. Despite its simplicity compared to modern computers, the Pascaline represents one of the earliest forms of a mechanical calculator, paving the way for the development of more complex computing machines.

94. ENIAC: The Giant that Changed the World

TECHNOLOGY AND INVENTIONS

In the 1940s, the Electronic Numerical Integrator and Computer, or ENIAC, was created and is considered one of the first true electronic computers. This colossal machine filled entire rooms and consumed vast amounts of electricity. It was capable of performing thousands of mathematical calculations per second—a feat that revolutionized how calculations were performed and applied in scientific and military endeavors.

95. Personal Computers: The Computer for All

The 1980s marked the era when personal computers (PCs) became widespread. These machines were small enough to fit on a desk and affordable enough for mass consumption. For the first time, families and individuals could enjoy the powers of computing at home, using PCs for writing, gaming, and other tasks, significantly enhancing productivity and entertainment.

96. Internet: The Network that Connects the World

The introduction of the Internet was a game-changer for computers, turning them from standalone computing machines into portals to a global network of information. Originally a project for military and academic purposes, the Internet was opened to the public in the 1990s and has since become integral to global communications, allowing instant access to information and real-time communication across the world.

97. The Microprocessor: A Revolution in a Chip

The invention of the microprocessor in 1971 was a monumental event in computer history. This tiny chip could perform the functions of an entire computer's central processing unit, which allowed for the production of smaller, faster, and more affordable computers. The microprocessor facilitated the widespread adoption of computers, making them accessible to the general public and integrating them into daily life.

DISTANCE COMMUNICATION

Long-distance communication has seen transformative changes over the centuries, evolving from rudimentary systems to sophisticated networks that connect us globally in real-time. Each technological leap has progressively shrunk the world, making it easier and quicker to share information across vast distances. Here's a look at how these technologies revolutionized the way we connect with each other:

98. The Telegraph: Signals that Connected the World

The telegraph, pioneered in the early 1800s, marked the advent of electronic communication. Using Morse code—a system of dots and dashes—messages were transmitted over wires from one station to another. This breakthrough drastically reduced the time it took to send messages over long distances, from days or weeks to mere minutes, effectively making the world feel a bit smaller and more connected.

99. The Telephone: Talking Across Wires

Invented by Alexander Graham Bell in 1876, the telephone introduced the ability to hear the voice of another person in real-time, regardless of the distance. This invention profoundly changed personal and business communication, making it possible to have direct and immediate conversations with someone miles away, thereby personalizing long-distance communication like never before.

100. The Radio: Voices Traveling in the Air

Radio technology, which emerged in the late 19th and was perfected in the early 20th century, enabled the wireless transmission of sounds, including voices and music. This medium broadened the scope of communication, allowing for real-time broadcasting to a wide audience simultaneously, thereby becoming a vital tool for mass communication, entertainment, and information dissemination.

101. Television: Images Dancing on the Screen

Television brought a visual dimension to electronic communication when it became widely available in the mid-20th century. For the first time, people could watch events unfold in real-time from their living rooms, whether they were historical moments, such as lunar landings, or everyday news. Television became a cultural phenomenon, offering a new way to experience and understand the world through moving images.

102. The Internet and the Mobile Phone: Global Connectivity at the Touch of a Finger

The introduction of the Internet and the proliferation of mobile phones have ushered in an era of unprecedented connectivity. The Internet allows for the instantaneous exchange of information and communication worldwide, while mobile phones make this access portable and constant. Together, they have created a globally connected society, enabling people to call, text, email, and browse the web from virtually anywhere, thereby redefining the boundaries of communication.

INNOVATIVE MATERIALS

Materials science is an exhilarating field, constantly pushing the boundaries of what is possible with new and innovative materials. These materials are not just improvements over their predecessors; they redefine how we use technology in everyday life. Here's a deeper look at some of the groundbreaking materials that could change our world.

103. Graphene: The Super Material

Graphene is a groundbreaking material in the truest sense, composed of a single layer of carbon atoms arranged in a two-dimensional honeycomb lattice. It's remarkably strong for its very light weight and boasts exceptional conductivity of electricity and heat, along with near-perfect transparency. These properties make it a candidate for a multitude of applications, ranging from creating flexible electronic devices, enhancing the efficiency of batteries and solar cells, to developing new medical technologies and water purification systems.

104. The Electronic Skin: Technological Touch

Electronic skin (e-skin) represents a significant advance in materials science, mimicking the sensitivity and versatility of human skin. This thin, flexible material can detect variations in pressure, temperature, and even texture. Potential applications include wearable health monitors that track vital signs and skin conditions in real time, and as an interface for prosthetic limbs to provide sensory feedback, significantly enhancing their functionality and user-friendliness.

105. Metals with Form Memory: Metal Magic

Shape memory alloys (SMAs) have the remarkable ability to return to their original form after being deformed when exposed to the right temperature. This unique property is extremely valuable in various applications, such as in aerospace for self-adjusting components and in medicine for minimally invasive devices like stents, which expand naturally at body temperature to support blood vessels without additional intervention.

106. Aerogel: The Phantom Material

Aerogel holds the title for being the lightest solid and is primarily made of air, trapped within a delicate silica structure that gives it incredible thermal insulating properties. Its uses extend from insulating space suits and spacecraft against the harsh conditions of space to potential applications in building highly efficient, lightweight insulation for homes. Aerogels could revolutionize architectural designs and energy savings, and they even have potential applications in cleaning up oil spills due to their absorbent nature.

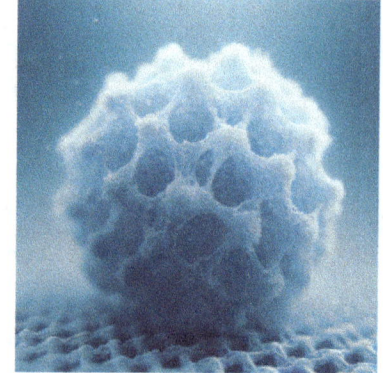

TECHNOLOGY AND INVENTIONS

VIRTUAL AND AUGMENTED REALITY

Virtual reality (VR) and augmented reality (AR) are groundbreaking technologies that dramatically enhance how we interact with the world and blend the digital with the real. By immersing users in entirely new environments or enriching the real world with digital overlays, VR and AR are reshaping entertainment, education, and commerce. Let's explore some exciting applications of these technologies.

107. Virtual Reality Helmets: Windows to Fantastic Worlds

Virtual reality helmets, or VR headsets, transport users to entirely new and fantastical environments. Whether it's exploring the depths of the ocean, walking on distant planets, or venturing into imaginative realms filled with mythical creatures, VR provides an immersive experience where the boundaries of reality are only limited by imagination. These helmets encapsulate your senses, allowing you to interact with and navigate these worlds in a way that feels real and tangible, making it a powerful tool for both entertainment and educational purposes.

108. Shopping with AR: Try Before You Buy

Augmented reality is transforming the retail experience by allowing consumers to 'try before they buy' in a completely new way. With AR, you can see how a piece of furniture fits in your room or how a dress looks on you without leaving your home. By pointing your smartphone's camera at a space, AR technology overlays digital images of products into real-world environments. This not only makes shopping more convenient but also helps in making more informed purchasing decisions, reducing the likelihood of returns and increasing customer satisfaction.

109. Augmented Reality Apps: Magical Overlays on the Real World

AR apps bring a layer of magic to everyday life by overlaying digital information onto the real world. Using your smartphone or tablet's camera, these apps can display educational content, entertainment, or practical information right before your eyes. Imagine walking through a park and seeing dinosaurs roaming around or looking up at the night sky to see stars annotated with names and information. AR apps can enhance learning, provide delightful experiences, and even assist with navigation and other practical tasks, making the environment around you interactive and informative.

QUIZ: TEST YOUR KNOWLEDGE OF TECHNOLOGY AND INVENTIONS

Question 11: What can a jetpack do?

- A) Navigating underwater
- B) Flying through the air
- C) Space travel
- D) Running at supersonic speed

Question 12: How do driverless cars work?

- A) Using printed maps to navigate
- B) Following a magnetic trail on the roads
- C) Using computers and sensors to see the environment
- D) Communicating telepathically with the driver

Question 13: What do we discover using customised underwater vehicles?

- A) Ancient wrecks and reefs
- B) New bird species
- C) Hidden caves on earth
- D) Stars and planets in the sky

Question 14: What innovations are attributed to Nikola Tesla?

- A) The light bulb and the phonograph
- B) Radio and wireless energy
- C) The telephone and telegraph
- D) The aeroplane and the jetpack

Question 15: What was one of Thomas Edison's major achievements?

- A) Invention of the telephone
- B) Bulb refinement
- C) Development of the first computer

TECHNOLOGY AND INVENTIONS

- D) Creation of the first aeroplane

Question 16: Why are Martian rovers important for science?

- A) They may take Martian soil samples
- B) Helping to understand whether there was life on Mars
- C) Exploring the Earth's ocean depths
- D) Monitor climate change on Earth

Question 17: What do rescue drones do?

- A) Putting out fires in dangerous areas
- B) They find and rescue people in emergency situations
- C) Delivering parcels to remote areas
- D) Photographing landscapes for detailed maps

Question 18: What is a function of robot surgeons?

- A) Perform surgery with incredible precision
- B) Assisting doctors in complex diagnoses
- C) Providing remote medical advice
- D) Managing hospital administration

Question 19: What does the Hyperloop enable?

- A) Travelling underwater without changing vehicles
- B) Move almost at aircraft speed
- C) Flying over city traffic
- D) Exploring the seabed

Question 20: What type of vehicle is an amphibious car?

- A) A vehicle that can fly and drive
- B) A vehicle that can drive on roads and navigate on water
- C) A vehicle that transforms into a submarine
- D) A vehicle that can explore Mars

ANSWERS:

- Question 11: B) Flying through the air

- Question 12: C) Using computers and sensors to see the environment
- Question 13: A) Ancient wrecks and reefs
- Question 14: B) Radio and wireless energy
- Question 15: B) Bulb refinement
- Question 16: B) Helping to understand whether there was life on Mars
- Question 17: B) They find and rescue people in emergency situations
- Question 18: A) Perform surgery with incredible precision
- Question 19: B) Move almost at aircraft speed
- Question 20: B) A vehicle that can drive on roads and navigate on water

HISTORY AND CULTURE

ADVENTURES IN TIME

Exploring history allows us to travel back in time and discover the fascinating ways in which ancient cultures and civilizations have shaped the modern world. From the architectural marvels of the Romans to the nomadic conquests of the Vikings, each civilization has left a lasting imprint on history. Let's embark on a journey through time to understand more about these remarkable cultures and their contributions.

110. The Roman Empire: The Conquerors of the Mediterranean

The Roman Empire, one of the most powerful civilizations in history, dominated a vast territory that stretched across three continents. The Romans were renowned for their architectural prowess, constructing enduring roads, aqueducts, and monumental structures like the Colosseum. These innovations not only facilitated the expansion and control of their empire but also laid the groundwork for modern engineering and urban planning.

111. The Vikings: The Navigators of the North

The Vikings, originating from Scandinavia, were both feared warriors and extraordinary seafarers. Their advanced navigational skills enabled them to traverse the harsh northern seas in their iconic longships, reaching as far as the Americas, which they called Vinland. The Viking sagas, rich with tales of exploration and conquest, continue to captivate and influence modern literature and culture.

112. Dinosaurs: The Giants of Prehistory

Dinosaurs, the preeminent rulers of Earth millions of years before humans, varied widely in shape and size. From the towering Brachiosaurus to the formidable Tyrannosaurus rex, these majestic creatures roamed diverse habitats across the globe. The study of dinosaurs helps scientists understand the evolutionary history of life on Earth and the processes that have shaped our planet's biological diversity.

113. Ancient Egypt: The Civilization of the Pyramids

Ancient Egypt, known for its incredible architectural achievements such as the pyramids and the Sphinx, was also a cradle of early scientific, mathematical, and medical knowledge. The Egyptians developed sophisticated methods of mummification to preserve bodies for the afterlife, reflecting their profound spiritual and religious beliefs, centered around an intricate pantheon of gods and goddesses.

114. The Great Wall of China: The Stone Dragon

HISTORY AND CULTURE

The Great Wall of China, a formidable fortification built to protect the Chinese states from invasions, stretches over 13,000 miles. Constructed by multiple dynasties over several centuries, the Wall is a testament to Chinese engineering and perseverance. It remains a symbol of national pride and is a monumental legacy of China's historical attempts to safeguard its civilization from external threats.

MYSTERIES OF LOST CIVILISATIONS

Lost civilizations spark our imagination with their secrets and mysteries, leaving behind enigmatic clues that have puzzled historians and archaeologists for centuries. Whether submerged under water, etched into the desert, or lost to flames, these ancient cultures captivate us with stories of human ingenuity and forgotten lore. Let's delve deeper into some of the most intriguing mysteries left by civilizations of the past.

115. Atlantis: The Lost City Under the Sea

The legend of Atlantis originates from Plato's dialogues, where he describes a technologically advanced civilization that vanished into the sea overnight due to a catastrophic event. The story of Atlantis has captured the imagination of countless generations, inspiring a myriad of theories about its existence and location. While some consider it a mythological teaching story, others continue their quest to uncover archaeological evidence that might prove the existence of this submerged city.

116. The Nazca: Enigmas from Heaven

The Nazca Lines, located in the arid plains of the Peruvian desert, remain one of the most profound archaeological enigmas. These vast geoglyphs, depicting various plants, animals, and geometric figures, are only fully appreciable from the air, suggesting a sophistication that baffles modern scientists. Theories about their purpose range from astronomical calendars to sacred pathways or even signs for water, yet their true function continues to elude definitive explanation, making them a fascinating subject of study and speculation.

117. The Library of Alexandria: The Lost Treasure of Knowledge

The Library of Alexandria, once the largest library of the ancient world, is famed for having housed an incomparable wealth of knowledge in the form of scrolls and books from across the known world. Lost to fires that occurred several times throughout its history, the exact location and the full extent of the texts it contained are unknown. The destruction of the library is one of the greatest cultural losses in human history, as it is believed to have contained works by some of the greatest thinkers and writers of the ancient world, including plays, poems, and scientific treatises that are now lost forever.

HISTORY AND CULTURE

WORLD HOLIDAYS

Holidays around the world offer fascinating insights into the cultures that celebrate them, each with its own set of traditions, rituals, and meanings. These special occasions bring communities together, showcasing a rich tapestry of history and beliefs through vibrant celebrations. Let's explore some of the world's most colorful and significant holidays and what makes them so unique.

118. Chinese New Year: The Festival of Dragons and Fireworks

Chinese New Year, or the Spring Festival, heralds the start of the lunar new year and is a major celebration across China and in Chinese communities worldwide. The festival is rich with symbolism and tradition, featuring lion dances, fireworks to ward off evil spirits, and a reunion dinner where families gather to share a meal of symbolic dishes such as dumplings, which represent wealth due to their shape resembling ancient Chinese money. Each year is linked to an animal of the Chinese zodiac, which influences the fortunes of the year ahead.

119. Diwali: The Festival of Lights

Diwali, celebrated by millions of Hindus, Sikhs, and Jains across the globe, is known as the Festival of Lights for its vibrant displays of oil lamps and fireworks that light up the night sky. This festival celebrates the triumph of light over darkness and good over evil, with families and communities joining together in prayer, festive feasting, and the exchange of sweets and gifts. Homes are decorated with colorful rangoli artworks, and candles and lamps are lit to invite the presence of Lakshmi, the goddess of wealth.

120. Hanukkah: The Jewish Celebration of Light

Hanukkah, also known as the Festival of Lights, is an eight-day Jewish holiday commemorating the rededication of the Second Temple in Jerusalem. According to tradition, the Jews witnessed a miracle when a day's supply of oil burned for eight days. To celebrate this, a menorah is lit, with one additional candle being lit each night until all eight are illuminated. Gifts are exchanged and foods fried in oil, such as latkes and sufganiyot, are enjoyed, symbolizing the oil from the miracle.

121. Rio Carnival: An Explosion of Colour and Music

The Rio Carnival is perhaps the most extravagant celebration in Brazil, famous worldwide for its exuberant parades and costumes, electrifying music, and spirited samba dancing. Samba schools prepare all year for elaborate performances and float displays that tell stories through dance, music, and visual art. The Carnival not only serves as a cultural showcase but also as a competition among the schools, with judges awarding prizes for music, costume, and float design.

122. Halloween: Night of the Witches

Halloween, celebrated on October 31st, has roots in the ancient Celtic festival of Samhain, when people would light bonfires and wear costumes to ward off ghosts. Today, it's known for trick-or-treating, jack-o'-lanterns, festive gatherings, and costumes. While it is largely a fun celebration characterized by spooky decorations and storytelling, it also retains elements of its harvest festival origins, with pumpkin carving and apple bobbing as popular activities.

ARCHAEOLOGICAL DISCOVERIES

Archaeology uncovers the layered stories of human history hidden beneath the earth, providing a tangible link to civilizations long past. Each discovery offers a glimpse into the ways people lived, worshipped, and interacted with their environment. Let's explore some of the most pivotal archaeological finds that have captivated scholars and the public alike, revealing secrets of ancient times.

123. The Tomb of Tutankhamun: The Treasure of Ancient Egypt

In 1922, Howard Carter's discovery of King Tutankhamun's tomb in Egypt's Valley of the Kings marked a milestone in archaeology, revealing a nearly intact royal burial filled with treasures. Despite Tutankhamun's relatively minor status as a pharaoh, his tomb's riches—such as his iconic gold funerary mask and the array of artifacts contained within—have provided invaluable insights into the burial practices, art, and everyday life of ancient Egypt.

124. Stonehenge: The Mysterious Circle

Stonehenge in England remains one of the world's most enigmatic prehistoric monuments. Composed of massive stones arranged in a circular setting, archaeologists believe it was constructed from 3000 BC to 2000 BC. Its purpose, possibly a temple for sun worship or a prehistoric cemetery, continues to be debated. The scale and precision of Stonehenge illustrate the sophisticated engineering skills of its builders and their deep connection to celestial phenomena.

125. The Dead Sea Scrolls: Ancient Scrolls of Mystery

The discovery of the Dead Sea Scrolls in caves near Qumran in 1947 dramatically expanded our understanding of early Judaism and the beginnings of Christianity. These texts, which include the oldest known Biblical manuscripts and other sectarian writings, shed light on religious practices and community life near the Dead Sea two millennia ago.

126. Discovering the Sassi of Matera

The Sassi di Matera, an ancient town carved from rock in Southern Italy, traces human habitation back to the Paleolithic period. Rediscovered in 1950 after being largely abandoned, Matera's cave dwellings reveal continuous human adaptation over 9,000 years. The town's recognition as a UNESCO World Heritage site and its designation as the European Capital of Culture in 2019 highlight its historical and cultural significance.

127. The City of Pompeii: A Moment Frozen in Time

Pompeii, once a thriving Roman city, was buried under volcanic ash from Mount Vesuvius in 79 AD. Rediscovered in 1748, the site provides an extraordinarily detailed snapshot of daily life in a Roman city. Preserved streets, homes, and public spaces offer insights into Roman architecture, commerce, and daily routines, while casts of volcanic ash victims poignantly evoke the human tragedy of the disaster.

128. Terracotta Warriors: The Underground Army of China

The Terracotta Army, discovered in 1974 near Xi'an, China, surrounds the burial complex of Emperor Qin Shi Huang, China's first emperor. This vast assembly of clay soldiers, each one distinct, was intended to protect the emperor in the afterlife. The warriors, along with horses and chariots,

and imperial power of the Qin Dynasty around 210 BC.

REVOLUTIONS THAT CHANGED THE WORLD

Revolutions have always been pivotal moments in human history, reshaping societies through sweeping changes that often lead to profound cultural, political, and economic shifts. From battles for independence to the digital transformation of societies, let's explore some of the most significant revolutions that have left lasting impacts on the world.

129. The American Revolution: The Struggle for Independence

The American Revolution was a seminal event that unfolded from 1775 to 1783, as the thirteen American colonies sought to free themselves from British rule. The colonists' demands for self-governance were fueled by grievances over taxation without representation and other forms of imperial control. Victory in this conflict led to the establishment of the United States of America, founded on principles of freedom and democracy as outlined in the Constitution. This revolution not only created a new nation but also inspired other countries toward self-determination.

130. The Industrial Revolution: The Change Machine

Beginning in the late 18th century in Britain, the Industrial Revolution marked a profound transformation from agrarian economies to industrial powerhouses. The introduction of machinery like the steam engine revolutionized production methods, particularly in textiles and manufacturing. This era saw a massive shift in population from rural areas to urban centers, sparking significant social and economic changes, including the rise of a factory-based economy and the expansion of new social classes.

131. The French Revolution: The Birth of Liberté, Égalité, Fraternité

The French Revolution, which started in 1789, was a radical and bloody upheaval against the longstanding monarchical and aristocratic structures in France. Driven by principles of liberty, equality, and fraternity, this revolution dismantled traditional power hierarchies, leading to the eventual rise of Napoleon Bonaparte. Its profound influence on law, society, and politics not only reshaped France but also inspired a wave of revolutionary movements across Europe and the world.

132. The Technological Revolution: The Information Age

The late 20th and early 21st centuries have been defined by the Technological Revolution, sometimes called the Digital Revolution. The widespread adoption of computers, the internet, and mobile technology has fundamentally altered daily life, communication, and commerce. This era has made information readily accessible, connecting the global community in unprecedented ways

HISTORY AND CULTURE

and fostering interconnectivity that transcends traditional boundaries. The impact of this revolution continues to evolve, driving innovations in virtually every aspect of society.

EMPIRES AND CONQUERORS

Empires throughout history have been instruments of immense cultural, military, and economic influence, shaping the world in ways that still resonate today. Led by formidable leaders whose names echo through the annals of history, these empires expanded their reach across continents, often leaving indelible marks on the societies they dominated or absorbed. Let's explore some of the most influential empires and their leaders who forged vast territories and left legacies that continue to impact our world.

133. Genghis Khan: The Steppe Warrior

Genghis Khan, the founder of the Mongol Empire, is renowned for his exceptional military strategies and leadership that led to the creation of the largest contiguous empire in history. His conquests spanned from China to Eastern Europe, encompassing vast regions under a single administrative framework. His policies promoted trade, cultural exchange, and connected diverse populations, facilitating a period known as the Pax Mongolica which significantly influenced trade and cultural life across Eurasia.

134. The Roman Empire: Ruling the Known World

The Roman Empire, epitomized by its first emperor Augustus, is one of the most iconic empires in history. At its zenith, it controlled vast territories across Europe, North Africa, and the Middle East, bringing Roman law, language, and engineering to these regions. The legacy of Roman governance, architecture, and the legal system has profoundly influenced Western civilization and continues to be the foundation of many modern legal codes and governmental structures.

135. Alexander the Great: The Conqueror Who United the World

Alexander the Great, king of Macedonia, was known for his unparalleled military achievements and the vast empire he amassed which stretched from Greece to Egypt and into northwest India. Alexander's conquests spread Greek culture throughout these regions, initiating the Hellenistic period which saw the mingling of Greek and Eastern cultures. His founding of numerous cities named Alexandria helped to cement his legacy as one of the greatest military tacticians and leaders in history.

136. The Ottoman Empire: A Bridge Between Continents

The Ottoman Empire served as a significant crossroads between East and West, Asia and Europe, over its six-century span. Founded by Osman I and reaching its apex under Suleiman the Magnificent, the empire is celebrated for its architectural achievements and the flourishing of arts, science, and religion. The Ottomans left a profound architectural heritage, including the Hagia Sophia and the Topkapi Palace, and were instrumental in the cultural and religious shaping of the region.

137. The British Empire: The Sun Never Sets

The British Empire was the largest empire in history and was often said to be the empire "on which the sun never sets." The empire exerted colossal influence over global politics, economics, and culture. The spread of the English language, British educational systems, legal practices, and other cultural norms across its colonies laid foundational aspects of many modern nations. Moreover, the empire's role in the global spread of industrial practices and technology set the stage for the modern global economy.

MONUMENTS AND WONDERS

Exploring the wonders of human ingenuity and creativity, we find remarkable monuments around the world that not only captivate our senses but also offer

HISTORY AND CULTURE

profound insights into the civilizations that built them. These architectural and engineering marvels serve as lasting testaments to human skill and vision, drawing millions of visitors each year who seek to connect with history in tangible ways. Let's delve into some of the most iconic and historically significant man-made wonders.

138. The Colosseum: The Arena of the Gladiators of Rome

The Colosseum, a symbol of the Roman Empire's grandeur, stands as one of the most awe-inspiring ancient structures in the world. Constructed during the reign of Emperor Vespasian, starting around AD 70, this amphitheater could hold up to 80,000 spectators and was the scene of gladiatorial combats, wild animal fights, and even mock naval battles. Its ingenious architectural design, featuring a complex system of vaults and arches, allows it to remain a blueprint for modern sports stadiums, showcasing the Romans' advanced engineering and understanding of crowd control.

139. The Taj Mahal: A Monument to Eternal Love

The Taj Mahal, located in Agra, India, is a mausoleum commissioned by Shah Jahan, the Mughal emperor, to house the tomb of his beloved wife Mumtaz Mahal. Completed in 1653, this stunning edifice is celebrated globally for its breathtaking beauty and intricate craftsmanship. Constructed from white marble inlaid with semi-precious stones and adorned with calligraphy, the Taj Mahal stands as a poignant symbol of love and a masterpiece of Islamic art and architecture.

140. Machu Picchu: The Lost City of the Incas

Perched high in the Andes Mountains, Machu Picchu is an iconic symbol of the Incan Empire. Often referred to as "The Lost City of the Incas," it was unknown to the outside world until its discovery by Hiram Bingham in 1911. This site features sophisticated dry-stone constructions that fuse huge blocks without the use of mortar, intriguing buildings that play on astronomical alignments, and panoramic vistas that speak to its strategic and ceremonial significance.

141. The Great Pyramid of Giza: An Ancient Egyptian Mystery

The Great Pyramid of Giza, built as a tomb for Pharaoh Khufu, is an architectural marvel that has stood the test of time for over four millennia. It was the tallest man-made structure in the world for nearly 3,800 years. What is particularly astonishing about the pyramid is not just its immense scale and enduring nature but also the precision with which it was constructed, aligned with the cardinal points of the compass with only minimal error. The pyramid's construction techniques remain a topic of debate and fascination among archaeologists and historians today.

CHARISMATIC LEADERS

Throughout history, charismatic leaders have emerged, captivating the hearts and minds of their contemporaries and leaving legacies that endure in memory and influence. These individuals, through their vision, courage, and unwavering determination, have navigated their nations through times of crisis and spearheaded movements that have reshaped societies. Let's delve into the lives and impacts of some of these remarkable leaders.

142. Cleopatra: The Last Queen of Egypt

Cleopatra VII, the last ruler of the Ptolemaic dynasty of Egypt, remains one of history's most fascinating figures. Known for her sharp intellect and political savvy, Cleopatra skillfully maneuvered through the treacherous waters of Roman politics to maintain Egypt's independence as long as possible. Her liaisons with powerful Roman figures like Julius Caesar and Mark Antony were as much political alliances as they were romantic, aimed at securing her throne and the future of Egypt. Cleopatra's reign epitomizes the complexities of female power in a male-dominated world and her legacy as a leader who fought relentlessly for her country's sovereignty continues to captivate historians and the public alike.

143. Nelson Mandela: The Freedom Fighter

Nelson Mandela stands as a symbol of freedom and reconciliation, not just in South Africa but around the globe. His long imprisonment and subsequent rise to South Africa's presidency encapsulate his commitment to justice and equality. As the first black president of South Africa, Mandela's leadership in dismantling the oppressive regime of apartheid and fostering a multi-racial democracy was marked by his advocacy for peace, understanding, and unity. His legacy is characterized by his unyielding resistance to injustice and his magnanimous approach to peace and reconciliation.

144. Gandhi: The Master of Peaceful Resistance

Mahatma Gandhi, often called the Father of the Nation in India, was pivotal in the struggle for Indian independence. His philosophy of non-violence, or Ahimsa, and his method of Satyagraha, or non-violent protest, influenced not

only the course of Indian history but also ignited movements for civil rights and freedom across the world. Gandhi's commitment to living a life of simplicity and integrity made his appeals to justice and human dignity all the more powerful and resonant, inspiring figures like Martin Luther King Jr. and Nelson Mandela.

145. Winston Churchill: The Lion of Britain

Winston Churchill is celebrated for his leadership during one of the most perilous times in British history, World War II. His tenure as Prime Minister is noted for his remarkable fortitude and resolve in the face of Nazi aggression. Churchill's speeches stirred the British public and provided them with the morale boost necessary to endure the war. His words and actions helped steer his nation through the darkness of war and into the light of victory, cementing his place as one of the great leaders of the 20th century.

GEOGRAPHICAL DISCOVERIES

Geographical exploration has long fascinated humanity, pushing the boundaries of known existence and facilitating encounters between diverse cultures. Throughout history, intrepid explorers have ventured into the unknown, charting new territories and expanding the global map. Their courageous journeys not only reshaped geographical knowledge but also set the stage for major political and economic shifts worldwide. Let's delve into the lives and expeditions of some of the most famous explorers who ventured far and wide, leaving a lasting legacy on world history.

146. Christopher Columbus: The Journey to the New World

Christopher Columbus, an Italian navigator sailing under the Spanish flag, famously crossed the Atlantic Ocean in 1492, aiming to find a western sea route to Asia. While not the first to discover the Americas—preceded by the Norse voyages to Greenland and Newfoundland and the indigenous peoples who had inhabited these lands for thousands of years—Columbus's voyages marked the beginning of sustained European interest and colonization in the New World. His expeditions opened up the Americas to European exploration and colonization, dramatically altering the course of world history through the Columbian Exchange and the massive transatlantic impact that followed.

147. Vasco da Gama: The Route to India

Vasco da Gama, a Portuguese explorer, achieved a monumental feat in the Age of Discovery by becoming the first European to reach India by sea, linking Europe and Asia via the ocean. His pioneering route around Africa's Cape of Good Hope in 1498 heralded a new era in global commerce, paving the way for an age of global imperialism and the establishment of the Portuguese Empire as a dominant trade power in Asia. Da Gama's voyages were instrumental in establishing a sea-based trade route that circumvented the previously arduous overland routes dominated by Middle Eastern and South Asian powers.

148. Marco Polo: The Merchant Who Mapped the Silk Road

Marco Polo, the Venetian explorer and merchant, is one of the most celebrated figures of the Middle Ages for his travels through Asia along the Silk Road. His detailed accounts of his journeys to China and his service at the court of Kublai Khan were published in "The Travels of Marco Polo," providing Europeans with their first comprehensive look at Asian lands and cultures. His descriptions of the wealth and vastness of China ignited interest in Asian trade and were an inspiration for countless explorers, including Christopher Columbus, who carried a copy of Polo's book on his voyages.

CODES AND LOST LANGUAGES

The quest to decipher lost languages and codes has always been more than an academic pursuit; it's a journey into the very thoughts and lives of ancient civilizations. Each successful decipherment not only expands our understanding of these cultures but also bridges the gap between the past and present, allowing us to hear the voices of peoples long gone. Let's delve into some of the pivotal linguistic breakthroughs that have unveiled rich histories and complex societies.

149. Egyptian Hieroglyphics: Secrets Engraved in Stone

Egyptian hieroglyphics are among the most iconic ancient scripts, recognizable for their intricate and artistic symbols depicting animals, gods, and daily activities. This writing system was used in Egypt for millennia, appearing on everything from monumental temple walls to delicate papyrus scrolls. The knowledge of how to read hieroglyphics was lost around the 4th century AD with the rise of Christianity and the decline of pagan cults. It wasn't until the discovery of the Rosetta Stone in 1799 and its subsequent decipherment by Jean-François Champollion in 1822 that scholars were able to unlock the vast records left by the pharaohs. Champollion's breakthrough provided unprecedented insights into Egyptian history, religion, and governance, rekindling interest in

Egyptology—a field that continues to yield archaeological and linguistic treasures.

150. The Cuneiform Scripture: The Ancient Voice of Mesopotamia

Cuneiform, developed by the ancient Sumerians of Mesopotamia, represents one of humanity's earliest writing systems. Unlike hieroglyphics, cuneiform was written by impressing wedge-shaped signs into clay tablets. Originally used for accounting and record-keeping, it evolved to document epic poetry, medical treatises, and royal decrees. This script was used across the ancient Near East for thousands of years by cultures including the Babylonians, Assyrians, and Persians. The decipherment of cuneiform began in the 19th century with the contributions of several scholars, notably Henry Rawlinson, who managed to translate the Behistun Inscription in Iran. Understanding cuneiform has opened a window into the political, economic, and religious life of these powerful early empires and has provided a direct connection to human civilization's first written expressions.

ANCIENT INVENTIONS

Ancient inventions are the bedrock upon which modern civilization has been built, showcasing the ingenuity and forward-thinking of our ancestors. From basic tools to complex systems, these innovations have had a profound impact on the development of societies around the world. Let's explore some of the most groundbreaking ancient inventions that have dramatically transformed human existence.

151. The Wheel: The Ride That Changed the World

The invention of the wheel around 3500 BC in Mesopotamia marked a pivotal turning point in human history. Initially used in pottery making, its adaptation for use in wheeled vehicles revolutionized transportation, enabling faster movement of goods and people. This invention facilitated trade and warfare, contributing to the expansion and interaction of civilizations. The wheel's principles are also foundational to modern machinery and transport, underscoring its lasting impact.

152. The Phonetic Alphabet: Words that Transform History

The development of the phonetic alphabet by the Phoenicians around 1050 BC was a revolutionary step in written communication. By using symbols to represent sounds rather than whole words or ideas, writing became more efficient and accessible, laying the groundwork for the spread of literacy and scholarly pursuits. The influence of the Phoenician alphabet extends through history, forming the basis of many contemporary writing systems including Greek and Latin, which in turn influenced numerous other global alphabets.

153. The Aqueduct: The Roman Masters of Water

Roman aqueducts, first constructed in 312 BC, exemplify ancient engineering prowess. These structures were designed to channel water from remote sources into cities and towns, supporting public baths, fountains, and private homes. The availability of fresh water had a tremendous impact on public health and urban development, allowing Roman cities to flourish and grow. The principles of Roman aqueducts influenced later developments in water management and are considered precursors to modern water supply systems.

154. The Solar Calendar: Measuring Time

The solar calendar, utilized by ancient civilizations such as the Egyptians and the Maya, was based on the sun's movement across the sky. This method of measuring time was crucial for agricultural planning, religious festivals, and administrative organization. By aligning their activities with the rhythms of nature, these calendars enabled societies to flourish agriculturally and culturally. The concept of time measurement remains integral to all aspects of modern life, from agriculture to the ways we organize work and leisure.

155. The Compass: Sailing Across the Seas

The perfection of the compass by the Chinese during the Song dynasty significantly advanced maritime navigation. By providing a reliable means to determine direction even when stars or landmarks were not visible, the compass enabled explorers to venture across vast oceans and into unknown

HISTORY AND CULTURE

territories. This tool was instrumental in the age of exploration, leading to the discovery of new lands and the integration of the world's economies and cultures.

QUIZ: TEST YOUR KNOWLEDGE ON HISTORY AND CULTURE

Question 21: What creatures dominated the Earth before the appearance of humans?

- A) Giant mammals of the Pleistocene
- B) Dinosaurs, prehistoric giants
- C) The first flying reptiles
- D) Large marine species of the Cambrian

Question 22: What was the main function of aqueducts during the Roman Empire?

- A) Illuminating the streets of Rome at night
- B) Transporting drinking water to cities from distant sources
- C) Decorating town squares to increase prestige
- D) Distributing wine during festivals

Question 23: What was the function of the Great Wall of China?

- A) Celebrating the emperor's greatness
- B) Observing the stars for astrological purposes
- C) Protect against external enemies
- D) Acting as a protected trade route

Question 24: For what purpose were the pyramids built in Egypt?

- A) As gift palaces
- B) As siege shelters
- C) As monumental tombs for the pharaohs
- D) As warehouses to store grain

Question 25: How did the compass influence maritime exploration?

- A) Anticipating weather conditions
- B) Indicating the position of the setting sun
- C) Providing precise direction even without visual landmarks
- D) Measuring the depth of ocean waters

Question 26: What information did the Dead Sea Scrolls provide?

- A) Plans of ancient lost cities
- B) Religious and historical texts that rewrote the biblical understanding
- C) Medical formulas for ancient cures
- D) Detailed star mapping

Question 27: What was the importance of solar calendars in ancient civilisations?

- A) Navigating deserts
- B) Calculating stellar positions for astrology
- C) Regulating seasonal agricultural practices
- D) Establishing dates for local markets

Question 28: What is considered the uniqueness of Terracotta Warriors?

- A) The vividness of their original colours
- B) Their uniformity of shape and size
- C) The individuality of each figure
- D) The use of precious materials in their construction

Question 29: What does the Taj Mahal represent?

- A) The military strength of the Mughal Empire
- B) A fortress against invasions
- C) A monument dedicated to eternal love
- D) An example of defensive architecture

Question 30: What was the most significant effect of the Industrial Revolution?

- A) The reduction of cities

- B) The reversal to the agricultural economic model
- C) The transformation from agricultural to industrialised economies
- D) The decrease in industrial production

ANSWERS:

- Question 21: B) Dinosaurs, prehistoric giants
- Question 22: B) Bringing drinking water into cities from distant sources
- Question 23: C) Protect against external enemies
- Question 24: C) As monumental tombs for the pharaohs
- Question 25: C) Providing a precise direction even without visual landmarks
- Question 26: B) Religious and historical texts that have rewritten the biblical understanding
- Question 27: C) Adjusting seasonal farming practices
- Question 28: C) The individuality of each figure
- Question 29: C) A monument dedicated to eternal love
- Question 30: C) The transformation from agricultural to industrialised economies

GEOGRAPHY AND PLACES

EXPLORERS OF LOST WORLDS

Exploration has always been a fundamental aspect of human curiosity, driving us to uncover the secrets of our planet's most mysterious and lesser-known places. These locales not only offer stunning natural beauty but also hold the keys to understanding ancient civilizations and the enduring myths that captivate our imaginations. Join me as we venture into some of the world's most fascinating sites, each with its own unique story and mystery.

156. The City of Petra: A Wonder Carved from the Rock

Petra, nestled in the rugged desert canyons and mountains of Jordan, is an archaeological and historical marvel. This ancient city, carved directly into vibrant red, pink, and orange sandstone cliffs, was once the thriving capital of the Nabatean kingdom. Petra's elaborate architecture and complex water conduit system highlight the advanced engineering skills of the Nabateans, who made the city a flourishing hub for trade routes that linked China, India, and southern Arabia with Egypt, Syria, Greece, and Rome. The city's most famous structure, the Treasury (Al-Khazneh), continues to awe visitors with its breathtaking precision and beauty, revealing the artistic and architectural prowess of its builders.

157. Loch Ness: Nessie's House

Loch Ness, located in the Scottish Highlands, is enveloped in mystery largely due to the legend of Nessie, the Loch Ness Monster. Beyond its mythical inhabitant, Loch Ness is one of the most extensive freshwater bodies in the UK, offering stunning scenery and a rich array of wildlife. The enduring legend of Nessie, first reported in 1933, has fascinated cryptozoologists and tourists alike, leading to numerous theories and expeditions aimed at uncovering the truth behind the sightings and bringing a blend of mystery and charm to this serene locale.

158. The Bermuda Triangle: Mystery by the Sea

The Bermuda Triangle, also known as the Devil's Triangle, covers an area of about 500,000 square miles of ocean off the southeastern tip of Florida. Renowned for its mysterious disappearances of ships and airplanes, the Bermuda Triangle has become synonymous with maritime mystery. While scientists and skeptics attribute the disappearances to natural phenomena such as methane hydrates or rogue waves, the triangle remains a popular subject of speculation and intrigue, drawing attention from around the globe.

159. Easter Island: The Stone Giants

Easter Island, or Rapa Nui, is one of the most remote inhabited islands in the world, located in the southeastern Pacific Ocean. It is renowned for its monumental statues called moai, created by the early Rapa Nui people. These towering figures are carved from the island's volcanic rock and dot the landscape, gazing inland across their former villages. The purpose and method of their construction remain subjects of scholarly debate, with theories ranging from ancestor worship to the  embodiment of political authority. The isolation and mysterious history of Easter Island continue to make it a compelling destination for historians, archaeologists, and travelers alike.

DESERTS AND THEIR SECRETS

Deserts, often perceived as barren expanses, actually teem with life and history, offering a treasure trove of scientific discoveries and ancient tales. These vast regions, each unique in its features and secrets, challenge the resilience of both life and human exploration. Let's delve into some of the most enigmatic and beautiful deserts on the planet and uncover the secrets they hold.

160. The Gobi Desert: Land of Dinosaurs

The Gobi Desert, stretching across northern China and southern Mongolia, is a paleontological hotspot, famous for its significant dinosaur fossils. Since the early 20th century, explorations have unearthed remarkable finds such as the first dinosaur eggs, providing insights into the prehistoric era. The extreme temperature fluctuations and sparse vegetation make the Gobi a formidable place, but its rich fossil beds continue to be a crucial source of scientific discoveries, shedding light on the creatures that roamed the Earth millions of years ago.

161. The Sahara: The Sand Giant

The Sahara Desert, covering most of North Africa, is synonymous with the classic image of a desert, with its expansive sand dunes and searing heat. Yet, it is also a place rich in history and culture. Rock art in regions like the Tassili n'Ajjer in Algeria offers a window into the lives of ancient peoples, depicting flora and fauna that suggest the Sahara was once a much wetter environment. Archaeological finds, such as the ruins of Roman cities and trade routes, tell stories of adaptation, survival, and connectivity in one of the harshest climates on Earth.

162. The Atacama Desert: The Driest Place on Earth

Chile's Atacama Desert, often referred to as the driest place on Earth, is so arid that some regions have never recorded rainfall. This extreme dryness makes it an excellent Earth analog for Mars, attracting scientists studying astrobiology and planetary geology. Despite its harsh conditions, life persists here in fascinating forms; microbial communities thrive in the soil, and specialized plants and animals have evolved mechanisms to capture and conserve water, demonstrating incredible adaptability.

163. The Antarctic Desert: The Silent Cold

Antarctica, primarily noted for its vast ice fields and brutal cold, is technically the world's largest desert due to its incredibly low moisture levels. The isolation and extreme environment make it an ideal location for studying a wide range of scientific subjects from climatology and glaciology to studying its unique biodiversity. Researchers here examine everything from ice cores that archive Earth's climate history to the peculiar life forms that inhabit this icy desert, offering critical insights into global environmental changes and Earth's ecosystems.

RAINFORESTS

Rainforests are critical to the ecological health of our planet. They are not only key regulators of the Earth's climate but also host to an astounding array of biodiversity. These vibrant ecosystems provide essential services, from carbon storage to maintaining the water cycle, and they offer profound lessons on ecological balance and biodiversity. Let's explore some of the most important rainforests around the world and discover their unique characteristics and the challenges they face.

164. The Amazon: The Green Lung of the Planet

The Amazon Rainforest, sprawling across nine countries in South America, is the largest and most biodiverse rainforest on Earth. It is often referred to as the planet's "lungs" because it produces more than 20% of the world's oxygen. This vast forest supports an incomprehensible variety of life, with millions of species of flora and fauna, many of which are still undocumented. The

Amazon is also home to over 400 indigenous tribes, each with their own rich cultures and deep knowledge of the forest. However, this vital ecosystem is under threat from deforestation, mining, and agriculture, which endanger its biodiversity and the global climate functions it supports.

165. The Rainforest of Congo: The African Heart

The Congo Basin, located in Central Africa, houses the world's second-largest rainforest, a critical part of the Earth's ecological balance. It plays a key role in regulating regional and global climate patterns and stores vast amounts of carbon. Rich in biodiversity, the Congo rainforest is home to iconic species such as the critically endangered mountain gorilla, forest elephants, and over 10,000 plant species, with new species frequently being discovered. Despite its ecological importance, this rainforest faces significant threats from logging, mining, and agricultural expansion.

166. The Borneo Rainforest: An Island of Biodiversity

Borneo's rainforest is one of the oldest in the world, estimated to be over 140 million years old. It is renowned for its incredible biodiversity, including many endemic species such as the endangered orangutan, the Bornean pygmy elephant, and the Sumatran rhino. This rainforest is a critical refuge for many species that are found nowhere else on the planet. However, Borneo has been experiencing one of the highest rates of deforestation in the world due to logging, illegal mining, and the expansion of palm oil plantations, which pose a severe risk to its ecological integrity and biodiversity.

MOUNTAINS AND THEIR MYSTERIES

Mountains have always evoked a sense of wonder and mystery, standing as natural giants towering over the landscapes they dominate. They are not only challenging physical frontiers for adventurers but also places rich in spiritual significance and mythical lore. Let's explore some of the world's most captivating mountains and the mysteries and legends they harbor.

167. Mount Fuji: Japan's Holy Mountain

Mount Fuji, an iconic symbol of Japan, rises gracefully with its almost perfectly symmetrical cone, capped with snow for several months of the year. Revered as a sacred mountain, it has been a pilgrimage site for centuries, drawing those who seek spiritual enlightenment through the act of climbing. The mountain appears frequently in Japanese art and poetry, symbolizing beauty and transient perfection. Each year, thousands climb Mount Fuji to witness the sunrise from its summit, an experience that holds deep cultural and religious significance.

168. Mount Everest: The Roof of the World

Mount Everest, known as Sagarmatha in Nepal and Chomolungma in Tibet, is not just the ultimate challenge for mountaineers; it is also a sacred entity in local folklore. The indigenous Sherpa people believe the mountain is the abode of a goddess, and traditional rituals are performed to seek her blessings for safety and success in climbing. Everest's towering presence and the extreme conditions faced by those who dare to ascend it contribute to its mystical allure and the legends that surround it.

169. The Rocky Mountains: The Great Backbone of North America

The Rocky Mountains, stretching across North America from Canada to New Mexico, are steeped in the history and lore of the Native American tribes, early explorers, and pioneers who traversed and settled the area. The Rockies are known for their breathtaking landscapes and diverse ecosystems. Legends of hidden gold mines, lost travelers, and sightings of mysterious creatures like Bigfoot pervade the folklore of the region, enhancing its mystique and drawing visitors and researchers interested in the paranormal and unexplained.

170. K2: The Wild Mountain

K2, often considered the mountaineer's mountain due to its demanding ascent and treacherous weather, holds a fearsome reputation. Known locally as the 'Savage Mountain,' K2 is surrounded by tales of spirits that guard it jealously. Unlike Everest, which has seen thousands reach its summit, K2 remains less trodden, its harsh conditions keeping many at bay. For the local Balti community, K2 is a site of reverence, and its unyielding nature is a reminder of the mountain's wild and indomitable spirit.

171. Kilimanjaro: The Mountain of Fire

Mount Kilimanjaro, the highest peak in Africa, is a dormant volcano that last erupted over 360,000 years ago. Known as the "Mountain of Fire," Kilimanjaro is surrounded by lush forests and diverse wildlife, making it a unique ecosystem. Local Chagga legends speak of spirits dwelling on the mountain, and many climbers have reported feeling a profound sense of awe and spirituality as they ascend its slopes. The mountain's shrinking glaciers and snow cap have also become a powerful symbol of the impacts of climate change.

RIVERS AND LAKES

Rivers and lakes are not just crucial sources of water and transportation; they are also steeped in cultural significance and enshrouded in mystery. These bodies of water have shaped civilizations, influenced cultures, and have been the setting for countless myths and legends. Let's delve into the stories and importance of some of the world's most famous rivers and lakes.

172. The Mississippi: The Artery of America

The Mississippi River, stretching about 2,320 miles (3,730 kilometers) from its source in northern Minnesota to the Gulf of Mexico, is deeply woven into the fabric of American history. It has been a major artery for trade, agriculture, and transportation, shaping the economic landscape of the United States. The river has also deeply influenced American culture, especially music genres like blues and jazz that echo the diverse cultures of people living along its banks. The Mississippi has been immortalized in literature and film, capturing the essence of America's evolution.

173. The Ganges: The Sacred River

The Ganges, known locally as Ganga, holds a special place in the hearts of millions of Hindus, who regard it as a mother and a goddess. It is believed that bathing in the Ganges helps wash away sins and facilitates Moksha, liberation from the cycle of life and death. The river supports millions of people living along its banks but faces severe pollution challenges, prompting significant environmental and health concerns. Balancing the river's spiritual significance with its ecological health is a major challenge for India.

174. The Nile: The River of Life

The Nile River has been Egypt's lifeline since ancient times, providing a fertile green valley across the desert landscape. It was so vital to the ancient Egyptians that they worshipped it as a god, Hapi, who was thought to bring the floods that fertilized their fields. Today, the Nile continues to be a crucial resource for agriculture and as a source of hydroelectric power. However, geopolitical tensions over water rights pose significant challenges to the nations along its banks.

175. Lake Baikal: The Siberian Giant

Lake Baikal, nestled in Siberia, is not only the deepest and oldest freshwater lake in the world, but it is also remarkably clear and biologically diverse. With thousands of species of plants and animals, many of which are endemic, it is often referred to as the 'Galápagos of Russia.' The lake is considered sacred by the local Buryat tribes who practice shamanism and is revered for its beauty and purity. Despite its remote location, environmental concerns such as pollution and climate change threaten its unique ecosystem.

UNINHABITABLE ZONES

Exploring the Earth's most uninhabitable zones provides not only a glimpse into the resilience of life but also insights into the adaptability of organisms in the face of extreme environmental conditions. These areas, though largely void of human habitation, are laboratories of evolution, showcasing how life can thrive under some of the most severe stresses imaginable. Let's delve deeper into some of the planet's most challenging environments.

GEOGRAPHY AND PLACES

176. Izu Island: Land of Poisonous Gases

Miyake Island, part of Japan's Izu archipelago, presents a stark example of nature's volatility. The island is characterized by regular volcanic activity, which emits hazardous levels of sulfur dioxide and other toxic gases. This persistent threat has led to repeated evacuations of the island's residents, rendering it temporarily uninhabitable. The situation on Miyake Island offers a unique opportunity to study the effects of volcanic gases on ecosystems and how certain plants and animals are able to withstand or even adapt to these harsh conditions.

177. Chernobyl: An Abandoned Land

The Chernobyl disaster in 1986 resulted in a massive release of radioactive material, transforming the surrounding area into one of the most notorious uninhabitable zones. However, the exclusion zone around Chernobyl has become a subject of intense scientific study, as wildlife populations, including wolves, bears, and wild horses, have not only returned but also thrived without human presence. This has provided researchers with valuable data on the ecological impact of radiation and the recuperative powers of nature when left undisturbed by human activities.

178. Antarctica: The Extreme Cold

Antarctica, the coldest place on Earth, challenges the very limits of life. The continent's extreme conditions — subzero temperatures, fierce winds, and almost complete lack of moisture — make it nearly uninhabitable for humans yet surprisingly hospitable for a variety of other organisms. Microbes, algae, and krill have not only adapted but have become integral to the Antarctic ecosystem. Research in these extreme conditions is crucial as it helps scientists understand the possibilities of life in similar environments, such as on Mars or other celestial bodies.

NATURAL MIRACLES

Our planet is a showcase of incredible natural phenomena, each highlighting the unique and dynamic processes that continue to shape our world. From the power of cascading waters to the enigmatic activities of geothermal areas and the vibrant life beneath our oceans, these natural miracles captivate and educate us about the delicate balance of our Earth's ecosystems. Let's explore some of these awe-inspiring natural wonders.

179. Niagara Falls: A Majestic Flow

Niagara Falls, straddling the border between the United States and Canada, is a testament to nature's raw power and beauty. Composed of three separate waterfalls — Horseshoe Falls, the American Falls, and Bridal Veil Falls — Niagara is renowned for its formidable volume of water that cascades over the precipice every second. This natural spectacle draws millions of visitors each year who come to witness its majesty. Beyond its visual splendor, Niagara Falls serves a practical purpose, providing vast amounts of hydroelectric power, which underscores the potential for natural resources to be harnessed in sustainable ways.

180. Yellowstone National Park: Land of Geysers and Volcanoes

Yellowstone National Park, the first national park in the U.S. and widely held as the first in the world, is an extraordinary region of geothermal activity. The park lies atop a volcanic hotspot, boasting more than 10,000 geothermal features including more than 500 geysers—half of the world's total. Its landscape is a vivid display of the Earth's internal forces, with geysers, hot springs, mudpots, and fumaroles. Yellowstone's unique geology not only provides a glimpse into the planet's dynamic nature but also supports a diverse range of wildlife, making it a critical habitat and a significant natural research laboratory.

181. The Great Barrier Reef: A Natural Aquarium

The Great Barrier Reef is one of the most spectacular marine ecosystems on the planet. Stretching over 2,300 kilometers, it is visible from space and comprises thousands of reefs and hundreds of islands made of over 600 types of hard and soft coral. This biodiversity hotspot is home to countless species of colorful fish, mollusks, starfish, turtles, dolphins, and sharks, among others. The reef also plays a crucial role in the marine environment, providing breeding and feeding grounds for many species. However, it faces significant threats from climate change, coral bleaching, and human activity, making conservation efforts vital for its survival.

ACTIVE VOLCANOES

Volcanoes are some of the most dynamic and visually stunning features of the Earth's surface, embodying both the creative and destructive power of nature. These geological formations not only play a crucial role in shaping the Earth's landscapes but also offer valuable insights into the processes that drive our planet's geology. Let's explore some of the world's most active and renowned volcanoes and the unique characteristics that make each of them fascinating.

182. The Kilauea: The Lava River of Hawaii

Kilauea, located in the Hawaiian Islands, is one of the most active volcanoes on Earth. This volcano is particularly famous for its vivid lava flows that stretch from the summit to the ocean, adding new layers of land to the island's coastline. These flows provide a rare opportunity for scientists and tourists alike to witness the ongoing process of land formation. Kilauea's eruptions are generally non-explosive but are spectacular displays of nature's ability to create and transform.

183. Vesuvius: The Guardian of Naples

Vesuvius is one of the most storied volcanoes in the world, infamous for its catastrophic eruption in 79 A.D. that buried the Roman cities of Pompeii and Herculaneum under a thick blanket of ash and pumice. Located in the densely populated region of Campania near Naples, Italy, Vesuvius poses significant risks to the local population. Its history and activity make it a key subject of study for volcanic monitoring and disaster preparedness strategies. Vesuvius remains a stark reminder of nature's sudden and devastating impact on human civilizations.

184. The Popocatépetl: The Giant of Mexico

Popocatépetl, affectionately known as "El Popo," is an active stratovolcano located just 70 kilometers from Mexico City, making its activity a matter of serious concern for the millions of nearby residents. It frequently emits gas, ash, and occasionally lava, and is one of the most closely monitored volcanoes in the world. The cultural significance of Popocatépetl in Mexico is profound, often featuring in folklore and regarded as a brother to the neighboring dormant volcano Iztaccíhuatl.

185. Mount Etna: Sicily's Mountain of Fire

Mount Etna, Europe's tallest and most active volcano, dominates the landscape of eastern Sicily, Italy. Known as "Mongibello," Etna is renowned for its almost constant state of activity, with frequent lava fountaining and ash emissions. Its eruptions provide spectacular natural fireworks but also pose threats to the local population. Etna's lava flows have created fertile volcanic soils that support extensive agriculture on its slopes, contributing to the region's renowned wine and fruit production.

GEOLOGICAL PHENOMENA

The Earth's surface is a dynamic and ever-changing canvas, shaped by a variety of geological phenomena that tell the story of our planet's past and present. These phenomena not only sculpt our landscapes but also significantly influence ecosystems, climate, and human civilizations. Let's delve into some of the most fascinating and educative geological phenomena that highlight the power and beauty of Earth's geological forces.

186. The Dolomites: Coral Mountains

The Dolomites, located in northeastern Italy, are renowned for their stunning beauty and distinctive pale mountains that captivate observers, especially at sunset when they turn a breathtaking shade of pink. This phenomenon, known as 'enrosadira', is a result of the unique composition of the Dolomite rock, which is rich in calcium carbonate and derived from ancient coral reefs. These mountains are a geological wonder, providing insights into the processes that can lift ancient seabeds to towering heights, offering a unique blend of ecological diversity and geological history.

187. The Rift Valley: The Scar of the Earth

The Great Rift Valley is a dramatic depression on Earth's surface, visible from space, that stretches approximately 6,000 kilometers from Lebanon to Mozambique. Its formation is a showcase of tectonic plate movements, where the Earth's crust is being pulled apart. This ongoing separation has created a series of rifts, volcanoes, and lakes, offering a live snapshot of continental drift in action. The Rift Valley is not only a geographical and geological wonder but also a biodiversity hotspot that supports a myriad of ecosystems across its length.

188. The Grand Canyon: A Natural History Book

The Grand Canyon, carved by the Colorado River in Arizona, USA, is a monumental testament to the power of water in shaping the landscape. The canyon exposes almost two billion years of Earth's geological history through its layered bands of colorful rock. Each layer tells a different story of Earth's past environments, from ancient rivers and tropical seas to vast deserts and lush wetlands. The Grand Canyon serves as a natural library, offering invaluable insights into geological processes and Earth's climatic shifts over millennia.

189. The Geysers of Yellowstone: Eruptions of Water and Steam

Yellowstone National Park is famous for its geothermal wonders, including over 500 geysers—more than half of all geysers in the world. These natural geysers, like the iconic Old Faithful, result from the intense volcanic activity beneath the park. The superheated water that erupts as steam and boiling water is a spectacular display of Earth's inner heat at work. Yellowstone's geothermal features are not only tourist attractions but also natural laboratories for studying the Earth's geothermal energy and the unique

GEOGRAPHY AND PLACES

ecosystems that arise around these hot springs.

QUIZ: TEST YOUR KNOWLEDGE OF GEOGRAPHY AND PLACES

Question 31: Where is the Bermuda Triangle?

- A) In the North Pacific
- B) In the North Atlantic
- C) In the Mediterranean Sea
- D) In the Red Sea

Question 32: What characterises the city of Petra?

- A) The pyramids
- B) Rock-cut structures
- C) Modern skyscrapers
- D) The Golden Temples

Question 33: What legendary creature is said to inhabit Loch Ness?

- A) A dragon
- B) A unicorn
- C) Nessie
- D) A Leviathan

Question 34: What do the statues on Easter Island represent?

- A) Sea gods
- B) Worshipped ancestors
- C) Warriors fallen in battle
- D) Fertility deities

Question 35: What is the main characteristic of the Sahara?

- A) It is a frozen desert
- B) It is the largest hot desert in the world
- C) It is completely lifeless
- D) It is the smallest desert in the world

Question 36: What makes the Atacama Desert unique?

- A) It is the wettest place on Earth
- B) It is known for its frequent rainfall
- C) It is considered the driest place on the planet
- D) It is full of lakes and rivers

Question 37: Why is Antarctica considered a desert?

- A) For its high temperatures
- B) Due to its low annual precipitation
- C) For its dense forests
- D) For its many animals

Question 38: What kind of biodiversity is the Amazon home to?

- A) Mainly marine species
- B) A wide variety of plants and animals
- C) Only a few species of trees
- D) None, it is completely sterile

Question 39: What role does Mount Fuji play in Japan?

- A) It is a popular tourist destination for winter holidays
- B) It is considered a sacred place and a national symbol
- C) It is known to be home to the oldest coal mines in Japan
- D) Used exclusively for geological scientific research

Question 40: Where is Yellowstone National Park located?

- A) In Australia
- B) In Europe
- C) In the United States
- D) In Asia

ANSWERS:

- Question 31: C) Interactions between the solar wind and the earth's magnetic field
- Question 31: B) In the North Atlantic
- Question 32: B) Rock-cut structures
- Question 33: C) Nessie
- Question 34: B) Worshipped ancestors
- Question 35: B) It is the largest hot desert in the world
- Question 36: C) It is considered the driest place on the planet
- Question 37: B) Due to its low annual precipitation
- Question 38: B) A wide variety of plants and animals
- Question 39: B) It is considered a sacred place and a national symbol
- Question 40: C) In the United States

WORLD RECORDS AND EXTRAORDINARY FACTS

NATURAL WORLD CHAMPIONS

The natural world is a stunning showcase of evolutionary extremes, with certain species demonstrating awe-inspiring features and abilities that hold records within the animal and plant kingdoms. These records not only highlight the diversity of life on Earth but also the extraordinary ways in which various organisms have adapted to their environments. Here are some of the most fascinating world champions of nature.

190. The Blue Whale: Giant of the Seas

The blue whale, the largest animal ever known to have lived on Earth, is a true giant of the seas. With an average length of 25 to 30 meters (82 to 98 feet) and weighing up to 200 tonnes, these marine mammals are larger than even the largest dinosaurs. Their hearts, which are the size of a small car, pump vast quantities of blood necessary to sustain their massive bodies. Blue whales roam the open seas, primarily in the Southern and Pacific Oceans, and their immense size is thought to be a result of the abundance of food in their deep-water habitats.

191. Rafflesia Arnoldii: The Biggest Flower

Rafflesia Arnoldii is notorious not just for its size, with flowers reaching over a meter in diameter, but also for its distinctive odor of decaying flesh. This smell attracts carrion flies that pollinate the plant. Native to the rainforests of Indonesia, the Rafflesia is a parasitic plant with no visible leaves, roots, or

stem, drawing all its nutrients from a host vine. The flower's dramatic appearance and lifecycle make it a biological curiosity and a symbol of exotic biodiversity.

192. The Giant Sequoia: The Titan of the Woods

Giant sequoias are among the most massive living organisms on Earth, with the ability to reach over 84 meters (275 feet) in height and more than 8 meters (26 feet) in diameter. Found primarily in the Sierra Nevada mountain range of California, these trees can live for thousands of years. The General Sherman tree, the largest of these, is not only a testament to the longevity of these trees but also to their resilience, surviving and thriving through countless natural challenges over centuries.

193. Devil's Claw: The Crab with the Strongest Grip

The coconut crab, also known as the devil's claw, possesses the strongest grip of any animal. This terrestrial crab, found on islands in the Indian and Pacific Oceans, can exert a force of over 1,600 newtons with its pincers. It uses this remarkable strength to crack open coconuts and other hard-shelled fruits, which form a significant part of its diet. This ability is crucial for its survival in the nutrient-sparse island environments where it lives.

UNBELIEVABLE BUT TRUE!

Our world is a treasure trove of oddities and marvels, with some phenomena so strange and spectacular that they seem almost unbelievable. These extraordinary facts not only challenge our understanding but also captivate our imagination, reminding us of the wonders that lie beyond the realm of everyday experience. Let's delve into some of these curious and almost mythical realities from around the globe.

194. The Boiling Lake

Located in Dominica, the Boiling Lake is an awe-inspiring natural wonder. Measuring roughly 200 feet across, this flooded fumarole, a crack in the Earth's surface which releases steam and gases, is the second-largest hot lake in the world. The water temperature on the edges can range from 82°C to 91.5°C (180°F to 197°F), but the center is actively boiling. The lake is enveloped in a cloud of vapor, and the surrounding area is often shrouded in mist, giving it a surreal appearance akin to a scene from a science fiction movie.

195. Rain of Fishes in Honduras

In the small town of Yoro, Honduras, an extraordinary meteorological phenomenon known as "Lluvia de Peces" occurs annually. Following severe thunderstorms, residents have reported fish falling from the sky. One theory suggests that tornado-like conditions over water bodies might lift the fish into the air and deposit them over land as the storm dissipates. This unusual event is celebrated with a festival and remains a subject of fascination and speculation among scientists and locals alike.

196. The Longest Natural Ice Tunnel

In the depths of Alaska's glaciers lies the world's longest natural ice tunnel, extending over 3 kilometers (nearly 2 miles). These tunnels form from the movement of meltwater underneath the glacier, which over time creates extensive subglacial channels. The sheer scale and beauty of these icy passages offer a unique glimpse into the dynamic processes at work beneath a glacier's surface, providing valuable insights into the nature of glacial movements and the impact of climate change.

197. The Flowering Desert

The Atacama Desert in Chile, known as the driest place on Earth, witnesses a miraculous transformation every few years. Following rare and unpredictable rainfalls, the desert blooms into a vibrant expanse of color. This phenomenon, known as "Desierto Florido," occurs when

dormant seeds in the desert soil suddenly germinate. The bloom includes numerous species of flowers, many unique to the Atacama, turning the usually stark landscape into a temporary garden of extraordinary beauty.

SPEED RECORDS

Speed, in its many forms, captivates and thrills, showcasing the pinnacle of performance across the natural world and human innovation. From the swiftest animals that race across the landscape to technological marvels designed to reach astounding velocities, let's explore some of the most remarkable speed records known today.

198. The Fastest Motorcycle

The Dodge Tomahawk, while more a concept than a practical vehicle, represents the zenith of motorcycle speed potential. With a theoretical top speed of 560 km/h (348 mph), this motorcycle is powered by a V10 engine similar to that used in the Dodge Viper. Although it has never been tested at this speed in a controlled environment, and it isn't street legal, the Tomahawk serves as a stunning example of what is possible when automotive engineering pushes the boundaries of speed.

199. The Cheetah: Fastest on Earth

The cheetah is nature's speedster, holding the title for the fastest land animal. Capable of sprinting up to 112 km/h (70 mph) in bursts covering distances up to 500 meters (1,640 feet), this incredible speed is a survival mechanism that allows it to catch fleet-footed prey such as gazelles. The cheetah's body is finely tuned for speed, with a lightweight frame, long legs, and a flexible spine that propels it forward with each stride, making it a marvel of biological engineering.

200. Usain Bolt: The Fastest Man on Earth

Usain Bolt, often called "Lightning Bolt," set the world record for the 100 meters with a stunning time of 9.58 seconds at the 2009 World Championships in Berlin. At his peak, Bolt reached a breathtaking speed of 44.72 km/h (27.8 mph), a figure that illustrates just how fast human beings can run. Bolt's record remains one of the most iconic moments in athletics, symbolizing peak human speed and the extreme limits of human athletic capabilities.

GIANTS OF NATURE

The natural world is filled with fascinating examples of gigantism, where species grow to extraordinary sizes that captivate the imagination. These giants of nature are not only awe-inspiring in their physical proportions but also offer insights into biological adaptability and ecological roles. Let's delve deeper into some of these incredible creatures, from prehistoric deer to modern-day colossi.

201. The Giant Irish Deer

The Giant Irish Deer, or Megaloceros giganteus, stood out from other deer species due to its enormous size and remarkable antlers that could span up to 4 meters across. Roaming the forests and grasslands of Europe and parts of Asia during the late Pleistocene, this deer is one of the most iconic examples of Ice Age megafauna. Its dramatic antlers were likely used in mating displays and combat with rivals. Although the species went extinct approximately 7,600 years ago, it continues to fascinate paleontologists and enthusiasts alike for its sheer magnificence.

202. The Honey Giant: The Titan Bee

Wallace's giant bee (Megachile pluto), named after the British naturalist Alfred Russel Wallace who first described it, is indeed a titan among bees. With its large body and wingspan, this bee is significantly larger than typical honeybees. Rediscovered in Indonesia after being thought extinct, Wallace's giant bee remains elusive, highlighting the challenges of conserving and studying wildlife in dense tropical forests.

203. The Gambia Giant Rat

The Gambian pouched rat is extraordinary not only for its size but also for its acute sense of smell, which allows it to be trained to detect landmines and tuberculosis. This giant rat is native to parts of sub-Saharan Africa and is a nocturnal creature that uses its pouches to carry food back to its burrow. The combination of its size and utility in humanitarian efforts makes it a unique example of how animals can interact with human activities in positive ways.

204. The Goliath Snail: A Creeping Colossus

The African giant snail, or Achatina achatina, is known for its impressive size, capable of reaching up to 30 cm in length. It is one of the fastest-growing snails and is known for its voracious appetite, able to consume a wide variety of plants. While fascinating as a species, the goliath snail is also considered a pest in non-native areas, where it can cause significant agricultural damage.

205. The Giant Rabbit of Flanders

The Flemish Giant rabbit is a strikingly large breed that has been around since the 16th century. Known for their gentle nature and soft fur, these rabbits can weigh over 10 kg, making them some of the largest rabbit breeds in existence. They require specific care due to their size but are beloved by rabbit enthusiasts for their friendly personalities and cuddly appearance.

UNIQUE ANIMALS

The animal kingdom is brimming with creatures that exhibit unique behaviors, fascinating adaptations, and extraordinary

skills. These animals not only captivate our imaginations but also challenge our understanding of what is possible in nature. Let's dive deeper into the lives of some of the world's most unique animals, each demonstrating remarkable traits that set them apart.

206. The Octopus Dumbo: Flying Under the Sea

The Dumbo octopus, named for its distinctive ear-like fins resembling those of Disney's beloved flying elephant, inhabits the ocean's depths, typically found at 3,000 to 4,000 meters below the surface. Unlike most species of octopus that live near the seabed, the Dumbo octopus spends its life in the midwater of the deep ocean. It uses its unique fins to propel through the water, giving the appearance of flying, while its tentacles aid in steering and manipulating objects. This deep-sea inhabitant is one of the rarest and least-studied due to its inaccessible habitat, making every sighting a valuable moment for marine biologists.

207. The Flying Serpent: The Dragon of the Woods

Flying snakes, found in the forests of Southeast Asia, possess an astonishing ability to glide from tree to tree. These snakes climb to the treetops and launch themselves into the air, flattening their bodies into a concave shape to catch the air, creating lift. They can glide for distances of up to 100 meters, steering and changing direction mid-air. This unique method of locomotion is not only a means of moving from place to place but also a predatory tactic and a way to escape threats.

208. The Blowfish: The Sea Artist

The pufferfish, or blowfish, is renowned for its ability to puff up into a ball, a defense mechanism that makes it larger and more difficult for predators to swallow. What is less commonly known is the male pufferfish's role as an underwater artist. To attract a mate, the male creates intricate, geometric patterns in the sand on the ocean floor. These "crop circles" of the sea are crafted with precise movements and can be over 2 meters in diameter. The complexity and beauty of these designs are crucial for attracting females and play a significant role in their mating rituals.

209. The Chameleon Panther: The Colour Changer

The panther chameleon, native to the tropical forests of Madagascar, is a striking example of adaptability and camouflage. These chameleons can dramatically change their color based on temperature, light, and emotional state. The color changes are facilitated by specialized cells, known as chromatophores, which contain different pigments, and iridophores, which reflect light, allowing them to communicate and blend into their environment effectively. This capability not only helps them in avoiding predators but also plays a crucial role during mating season to attract partners or deter rivals.

PRODIGIES OF NATURE

Nature is indeed a masterful creator, constantly surprising us with phenomena and creatures that stretch the limits of our understanding. These marvels showcase not only the beauty and complexity of the natural world but also highlight its incredible adaptability and interconnectedness. Let's explore a couple of these prodigies that represent the extraordinary capabilities and phenomena of nature.

210. The Immortal Jellyfish

Turritopsis dohrnii, known as the immortal jellyfish, presents one of the most fascinating biological phenomena in the natural world: biological immortality. After reaching sexual maturity, this small, transparent jellyfish can revert to its polyp stage, essentially starting its life cycle anew. This process, known as transdifferentiation, involves the transformation of mature cells back into a juvenile form, allowing the jellyfish to bypass death, barring predation or disease.  This unique survival strategy offers scientists valuable insights into cellular regeneration and aging, with potential implications for medical research in humans.

211. Birds Dancing in the Sky

Murmurations of starlings are one of nature's most spectacular displays, where thousands, or even millions, of birds dance in the sky in a mesmerizing, highly coordinated performance. This phenomenon occurs primarily during dusk, as the starlings prepare to roost for the night. Scientists believe that murmurations serve several functions: they provide safety in numbers from predators, help the birds to share information, such as the location of feeding sites, and contribute to temperature regulation before nightfall. The intricate patterns and rapid movements of the murmuration, achieved through split-second timing and cohesion, remain one of the great wonders of natural choreography.

EXCEPTIONAL HUMAN SKILLS

Human potential is vast and varied, with some individuals exhibiting abilities that are nothing short of astonishing. These exceptional skills, whether inborn or honed through years of practice, highlight the remarkable adaptability and capability of the human body and mind. Let's delve into some of these incredible human abilities that showcase what individuals can achieve through either genetic gift, sheer will, or intensive training.

212. Human Computers: Math Geniuses

Individuals known as "human calculators" possess the extraordinary ability to perform complex mathematical calculations in their heads, often faster than someone could with a physical calculator. These individuals can handle large numbers, solve complex equations, and perform intricate calculations involving roots and exponentials effortlessly. This remarkable skill often stems from an innate ability combined with extensive practice and is sometimes associated with savant syndrome, where a person has profound capacities or abilities despite significant mental or physical disabilities.

213. Photographic Memory: The Living Archive

Eidetic memory, more commonly referred to as photographic memory, is a phenomenon wherein individuals can recall vast amounts of visual information in great detail, even after only brief exposure to it. People with eidetic memory can often vividly describe a scene or page from a book, recall intricate details of an event, or reproduce something they have seen once with astonishing accuracy. This ability is extremely rare and not fully understood, making it a subject of fascination and extensive study within the field of cognitive science.

214. Hyper-Flexibility: The Contortionism Artists

Hyper-flexibility, or extreme joint flexibility, is another fascinating human ability. Often showcased by contortionists in circuses and performance art, these individuals can bend and twist their bodies into positions that seem physically impossible for most. This ability is due to variations in connective tissues that increase their joints' range of motion. While some degree of this flexibility is innate, professional contortionists also undergo rigorous and specialized training to enhance their flexibility and control, turning their natural predisposition into an art form.

WORLD RECORDS AND EXTRAORDINARY FACTS

ACTS OF MAGIC AND ILLUSIONISM

Magic and illusionism tap into the human fascination with the mysterious and the seemingly impossible, captivating audiences around the world with performances that defy logic and reality. These magicians and illusionists have mastered the art of deception, using a blend of technique, psychology, and showmanship to create unforgettable moments. Here's a closer look at some of the most iconic magic tricks that have left audiences spellbound.

215. The Walk on the Great Wall of China

David Copperfield's 1986 performance where he appeared to walk through the Great Wall of China is one of the most talked-about illusions in magic history. This feat was achieved through clever staging, misdirection, and the use of technology, all orchestrated to perfection. The illusion involved Copperfield entering a small tent erected against the wall and, after a dramatic presentation, emerging from a similar setup on the opposite side of the wall. The spectacle left both live spectators and television viewers in awe, wondering about the secrets behind his mysterious passage through solid stone.

216. The Disappearance of the Statue of Liberty

David Copperfield's 1983 illusion, making the Statue of Liberty disappear, remains one of the most audacious magic tricks ever televised. The trick used strategic lighting, a giant rotating stage, and synchronized movements to obscure the audience's view momentarily, creating the illusion that the iconic monument had vanished. This performance not only showcased Copperfield's ingenuity but also his ability to execute a large-scale illusion that remains a benchmark in the world of magic.

217. The Impossible Escape

Harry Houdini's name has become synonymous with escape artistry, thanks to his daring and often dangerous acts of escape from handcuffs, straitjackets, and locked containers. One of his most impressive feats was escaping from a locked prison cell, which he claimed to accomplish using hidden tools and an in-depth knowledge of locks. Houdini's performances not only demonstrated his physical prowess but also his unmatched skill in turning escape artistry into a compelling form of entertainment.

218. The Man Who Walks on Water

In a modern display of illusionism, British magician Dynamo stunned onlookers by apparently walking across the River Thames. This illusion involved a hidden structure just beneath the water's surface, along with careful camera angles and crowd control, allowing him to appear as if he was walking on the water. This act captured the public's imagination and is a testament to how contemporary illusionists continue to innovate and captivate audiences with new twists on classic magic concepts.

REVOLUTIONARY SCIENTIFIC DISCOVERIES

Scientific discoveries are the milestones that have profoundly reshaped human understanding and opened up infinite possibilities and new realms of inquiry. Each breakthrough has not only broadened our knowledge but also profoundly impacted practical aspects of daily life, technology, and how we perceive our universe. Here's a closer look at some of the pivotal discoveries that have revolutionized science.

219. The Discovery of DNA

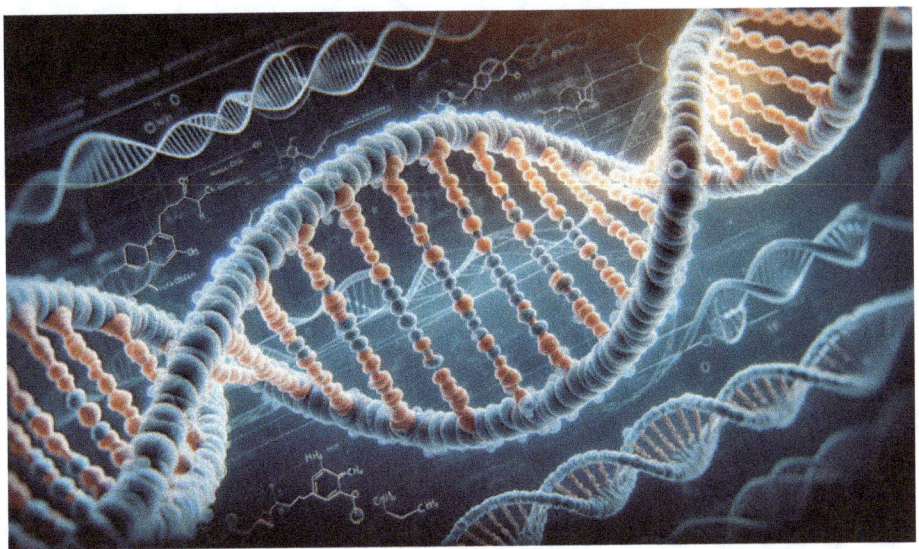

The identification of the structure of DNA by James Watson and Francis Crick in 1953 marked a monumental milestone in the field of biology and genetics. By elucidating the double helix structure of DNA, they unlocked the secret of genetic encoding, explaining how genetic information is stored and replicated. This breakthrough laid the foundation for genetic engineering, cloning, forensic science, and biotechnology, profoundly affecting medicine and agriculture by enabling genetic modifications that can lead to disease resistance and improved health outcomes.

220. Einstein's Theory of Relativity

Albert Einstein's Theory of Special Relativity, introduced in 1905, was a groundbreaking revelation that transformed the fields of physics and cosmology. The theory proposed that the laws of physics are the same for all non-accelerating observers, and that the speed of light within a vacuum is the same no matter the speed at which an observer travels. This insight led to the famous equation $E=mc^2$, which implies that energy and mass are interchangeable. This fundamental principle has numerous applications, including nuclear energy and our understanding of cosmic phenomena. It also paved the way for the General Theory of Relativity, which introduced the concept of gravity as the warping of space-time by mass and energy.

221. The Discovery of Extrasolar Planets

INCREDIBLE CURIOSITIES - THE GREAT ATLAS OF WORLD MYSTERIES

The confirmation of the first extrasolar planet orbiting a Sun-like star in 1995 by Michel Mayor and Didier Queloz revolutionized astronomy by confirming that our solar system is not unique in the universe. This discovery has since led to the identification of thousands of other exoplanets, expanding our understanding of the universe and enhancing the search for extraterrestrial life. The study of these distant worlds helps astronomers learn more about planetary formation and the potential habitability of other systems, which could be crucial for future interstellar exploration.

QUIZ: TEST YOUR KNOWLEDGE OF WORLD RECORDS AND EXTRAORDINARY FACTS

Question 41: How long can a blue whale reach?

- A) 50 metres
- B) 30 metres
- C) 20 metres
- D) 15 metres

Question 42: What does the Rafflesia Arnoldii flower smell like?

- A) Scent of a rose
- B) Smell of rotten meat
- C) Lavender fragrance
- D) No odour

Question 43: Which creature has the strongest grip of all animals?

- A) The lion
- B) The Coconut Crab
- C) The bald eagle
- D) The crocodile

Question 44: What natural phenomenon turns the Atacama Desert into a carpet of flowers?

- A) Annual strong wind
- B) Unusual rainfall every 5-7 years
- C) Heavy snowfall
- D) Volcanic eruptions

WORLD RECORDS AND EXTRAORDINARY FACTS

Question 45: Where does the 'Rain of Fish' phenomenon occur?

- A) In India
- B) In Honduras
- C) In Norway
- D) In Australia

Question 46: What maximum speed can the cheetah reach?

- A) 90 km/h
- B) 101 km/h
- C) 112 km/h
- D) 120 km/h

Question 47: What is Usain Bolt's world record in the 100 metres flat?

- A) 9.58 seconds
- B) 9.68 seconds
- C) 9.72 seconds
- D) 9.83 seconds

Question 48: How long can the African goliath snail grow?

- A) 15 cm
- B) 20 cm
- C) 25 cm
- D) 30 cm

Question 49: What makes the Dumbo octopus unique?

- A) The ability to change colour quickly
- B) Fins resembling ears
- C) The ability to emit bioluminescence
- D) Swimming speed

Question 50: What is the special characteristic of the flying snake?

- A) Can run at 40 km/h
- B) It has a deadly poison
- C) Can glide between trees

- D) It is completely aquatic

ANSWERS:

- Question 41: B) 30 metres
- Question 42: B) Smell of rotten meat
- Question 43: B) The Coconut crab
- Question 44: B) Unusual rainfall every 5-7 years
- Question 45: B) In Honduras
- Question 46: C) 112 km/h
- Question 47: A) 9.58 seconds
- Question 48: D) 30 cm
- Question 49: B) Fins resembling ears
- Question 50: C) It can glide between trees

CONCLUSION: BEYOND THE HORIZON

Dear young adventurers,

As we draw the curtains on this incredible voyage of discovery and knowledge, I want to leave you with some essential tools and insights that will guide you as you continue to explore the vast universe of learning.

Learning to Learn

Your curiosity is your compass, and knowledge is your rudder. Mastering the art of learning is perhaps the most crucial skill you can develop. Always dig deeper:

Ask Questions: Enhance the quality of the answers you find by asking thoughtful and probing questions. Stay inquisitive, always pondering "Why?" and "How?".

Think Critically: Scrutinize sources, evaluate facts, and form your own opinions. Critical thinking shields you from misinformation and myths.

Apply What You Learn: Transform knowledge from abstract to practical. Use what you discover to innovate, solve problems, and enrich your life and those around you.

Preserving the Wonder

Wonder is the core of childhood curiosity and should be cherished and nurtured well into adulthood. Here's how you can keep that spark alive:

Explore Nature: Venture outdoors. The natural world is a living laboratory brimming with lessons on everything from biology to physics.

Read Voraciously: Books are gateways to vast new worlds, each one offering fresh insights and adventures. Every book you open expands your mind further.

Share Your Knowledge: The act of teaching is a powerful method of learning. When you share your knowledge, you not only enlighten others, but you also reinforce and broaden your own understanding.

Acting with Responsibility

With great knowledge comes great responsibility. Use your insights and discoveries for the greater good:

Be a Guardian of the Planet: Every decision and action has an impact. Make choices that support sustainability and protect our world.

Participate and Make an Impact: Engage in your community and the world— whether through science, politics, education, or the arts. Even small actions can lead to significant changes.

Inspire Others: As explorers of knowledge, you have the power to motivate those around you. Share your stories, present facts, and invite others to join you on this endless journey of discovery.

Continue Exploring

Remember, every chapter's end is just the start of a new adventure. This is not goodbye, but rather an encouragement to keep seeking, learning, and dreaming. The world is a mosaic of mysteries waiting to be uncovered. May the pages you've turned equip you for the exciting explorations to come.

Happy exploring, young adventurers! The path ahead is rich with wonders waiting for you to decode them. Keep your curiosity alive, and let it lead you to extraordinary places.

www.ingramcontent.com/pod-product-compliance
Lightning Source LLC
Chambersburg PA
CBHW072212070526
44585CB00015B/1300